OPEN UP THE WALL

OPEN UP THE WALL

Revelations of a Renovation Contractor

GEOFF BOWES

Willanna Publishing
Toronto

OPEN UP THE WALL

Revelations of a Renovation Contractor

Copyright © 2018 by Geoff Bowes

All rights reserved. This book or any portion thereof may not be reproduced or used in any manner whatsoever without the express written permission of the publisher except for the use of brief quotations in a book review.

Paperback Edition ISBN: 978-1-7750164-1-0

Printed by CreateSpace

openupthewall.com

Willanna Publishing

105 - 35 Boardwalk Drive
Toronto, Ontario, Canada M4L 3Y8

Cover design: Will Bowes   Interior design: Tim Reilly

To tradespeople everywhere

The circular saw is a beautiful, versatile machine. It is the daily workhorse of the construction industry. Hand held, a relationship naturally grows between the tool and its owner. From start to finish, it sounds reluctant to do the carpenter's bidding. It starts up at full volume screaming "WATCH YOUR FINGERS!!!" and ends with a diminuendo sigh of "Thank God that's over."

Table of Contents

Introduction	11
One: Coming Out	13
Two: Weekend Warrior	18
Three: Stiffed	29
Four: The New World	37
Five: Fitting In	49
Six: Homework	56
Seven: Know Your Place	64
Eight: Working Relationship	67
Nine: A Poor Choice	73
Ten: The Real Deal	78
Eleven: Finding Purpose	89
Twelve: Legitimate Business	94
Thirteen: Hey, It's Christmas	101
Fourteen: Happy New Year	109
Fifteen: The Addition of Death	113
Sixteen: No Turning Back	120
Seventeen: The Help	129
Eighteen: The Entitled	143
Nineteen: Know When to Fold 'Em	151
Twenty: The Addition of Life	163
Twenty-One: The Addition of Discovery	177
Twenty-Two: Missing the Turn	200
Twenty-Three: Something Gives	209
Twenty-Four: Recovery	213
Twenty-Five: Bloody Hell	216
Twenty-Six: Process of Elimination	226
Twenty-Seven: Going South	229
Acknowledgements	237
About the Author	239

Introduction

There is a question that renovation contractors are frequently asked:
"Can't you just cover it over?"
My answer to my clients has to be: "No."
Cover over, gloss over, overlook – they all mean denial. My job is to make clients understand that in order to do a safe and solid renovation, I must be able to see what is working, what isn't, and what has to change. The only way to do that is to tear out a wall, or cut open a ceiling, and cover everything they own in a fine dust.
The next question is, of course: "How much will it cost me?"
It will cost you money, anxiety, disruption of routine, more money, sleepless nights, fear of failure, and fear of miscommunication. For however long it takes,your life will be controlled by guys in toolbelts. This means that at any point in the renovation process, walls can fly up to protect hurt feelings, shield resentment, or simply hide confusion. These are the ones that have to get opened up first.
This book is about the walls that I opened up, and the walls that opened up for me when I changed careers and attitude, bought a toolbelt, and entered the fascinating, fraught, risky, and rewarding world of the construction business.
But it isn't about business. It's about the crazy extreme personalities that taught me the business, and the crazy

extreme homeowners that we do business with. This book is about what you don't see on TV reno shows - class discrimination, personal triumph, physical pain, and loyalty. While there are humorous accounts of bloody injury, naked confrontation and one memorable sexual assault by a big dog, my purpose in writing this book is to give insight into life on my side of the toolbelt, and to celebrate all the talented people who come into our homes and forever change the way we live.

One: Coming Out

I remember the day that started the change in my life. The most inconsequential details of that day have stayed clear in my memory, like the note in the breast pocket of my denim shirt reminding me to pick up milk, and the bit of celery between my teeth.

It was the day that I walked into a hardware store to buy my first power tool.

This was in 1981, back when Wayne Gretzky had a mullet, long before renovation was a household word, and years before the Home Depot had been conceived. It was back when items like power saws and drills were kept behind the counter at the Hardware Store, along with guns and ammo.

I waited until the counter was clear of customers and then approached the kindly pensioner on the other side and said, "I'd like to buy an electric saw."

"OK, you want a Skil saw? Jigsaw? Table saw?"

"Well, I have to cut the ends off some boards, so I was thinking about the hand-held kind with the round blade."

"Circular saw. Mostly called a Skil saw."

"Yes, that's what I'm after, a Skil saw."

Then I said: "The thing is, I'm not good with my hands, so if there is one that's safer than the others, I should probably get that one."

"There's no such thing as a safe power saw," warned the man. "Every one of them is dangerous as hell, so if you're not good with your hands, well, maybe you should hire someone else to do the cutting for you."

My face flushed. "YOU'RE NOT GOOD WITH YOUR HANDS" proclaimed by a stranger made me very angry, very quickly. It wasn't a bruised ego type of angry; it was a hurt angry, a reaction to some old pain, some ... shame?

"I'm not a complete idiot!" I snapped.

The clerk put his hands across his chest in a protective way. "What did I say?" he asked. A vein pulsed on his temple.

"Nothing. Never mind." I smacked my hand on the Skil saw. "This one. I'll take this one."

We completed the transaction in silence. I wanted to apologize to the man for being ... weird, but I couldn't think of an explanation for my behaviour, other than "You made me feel ashamed of myself." So I just thanked him as though nothing out of the ordinary had happened and left.

The box had the SKIL logo on it in orange letters. The identical SKIL decal was on the glass door to the shop class in my middle school. I never went through that door because I wasn't allowed to take shop, because everybody in our family knew that "GEOFFREY IS NOT GOOD WITH HIS HANDS."

Now, sitting in the kitchen of my half-renovated house, staring at the SKIL logo on the unopened box, I came to understand my reaction to hearing that out loud.

"Geoffrey is not good with his hands" had been an unchallenged truth for as long as I can remember, but I could not recall a single event that gave any credence to this fable of my manual ineptitude.

Open Up The Wall

I remember being warned on a few occasions that tools were for 'common people', and that if I didn't study hard and get good marks I would end up a 'common tradesman'. When I volunteered to replace the deadbolt on the shed door, the idea was scoffed at and my mother gave the job to the gardener, her assumption being that all common tradesmen knew everything about all common trades.

Mother spent considerable time directing me away me from a life of common industry. Instead of shop, Geoffrey took violin.

Geoffrey. The very name is pretentious.

Geoffreys wear blazers. They pass sandwiches. They listen to Coldplay. They don't own work boots. And they stay well away from power tools.

Memories of feeling inadequate around boys who built birdhouses and cheese boards in shop class came flooding back as I sat on my pile of floor boards, holding my new saw by the cord.

When I first had the idea to put a pine floor in the living room, I felt a genuine urge to do the work by myself. Back in those days, such an undertaking would be regarded as an unusual thing to do, and there would have been nosey neighbours thinking "Oh my God, he's working on his own house! He must be TOO POOR to hire somebody." None of this mattered to me. I was ready to put my hands to the test and discover what not being good with them was all about.

As I loaded the lumber into the house, I couldn't help but admire every board. Each one had a unique and colourful grain, and each grain was beautiful in its detail. I followed their route down the length of the board with my finger and decided on the placement of each one. It was a creative, calming, and altogether uncommon experience. I lingered over my choices, well aware that I was postponing the inevitable — cutting the boards to the right length with my new SKIL saw, the tool that I had never touched in my well-bred life. I rummaged through the box for instructions, but of course there were none because ... what's to know? Basically a SKIL saw is like a hairdryer — plug it in, turn it on and it does what it's supposed to do, be it blow hot air or spin a disk with 28 razor-sharp teeth on it.

I picked it up, feeling like the guy tied to the rack while the torturer waves a hot poker in front of him — the dread is not so much in the visual as it is in the imagination of what is to come. I have a vivid imagination, so before it could take off with gory images of my amputated hand, I plugged in the saw and very carefully got to work. When I pulled the trigger, the saw screamed at me. I jumped. This was no longer the distant sound of a construction site; this was close, loud and shocking. This was my saw, my event, and there was no turning back.

One board at a time. Measure, draw a line across the board, and cut on the line without wavering. Thirty-seven cuts. I kept waiting to feel like I was getting the hang of it, but the shriek of the saw unnerved me with every cut, and the best I could think of this terrifying machine was that it was a necessary evil. I felt out of myself, watching ME using a power saw. Sweat gathered on my upper lip in anticipation of a horrible bloody accident. At the halfway point, I had convinced myself that I was not cut out for this aspect of manual labour and resolved to try and return the saw as soon as the last board was cut. The whole enterprise was way too scary for me.

Open Up The Wall

Except ...

Nearly seven and a half hours later, I nailed down what was to me the most beautiful pine floor in all the land. Finally finished, I lay face down on my creation and let the smell of fresh-cut softwood linger in my nose while I stroked along the grain. I had done good things with my hands, and I still had all my fingers. I had joy.

I raised my chin off the floor and there in the corner at eye level, was my SKIL saw.

Lying on its side with the half moon blade guard pointing up, the saw was smiling at me.

Two: Weekend Warrior

The word renovation had come into my vocabulary about the time that I purchased my first house, a rundown "starter home." I was part of the first wave of yuppies who began buying up older homes and turning them into "open concept" caverns back in the 1980s. We stripped the paint off the old trim to expose the natural wood. We took out pink and black bathroom tile and replaced it with white tiles. We did white walls, white ceilings, white appliances, and even white carpet. White everything, except for the hand-stripped door and window trim.

I was right in there with my vision of a renovated home, all woody and white and perfect. What clouded this vision was the mysterious collection of pipes and wires that filled the basement ceiling. The home inspector had pulled on the wires, and banged the pipes, and nodded approvingly. I wanted to be like him. I wanted to look at the ceiling and understand what I was looking at. Everybody knows that copper pipes are for water, and the really big tin ones are for heat, but what about the black ones? You can hear water gurgling through them, and they appear to be made of plastic! One good bang, and they might crack like a cold yogurt cup and disgorge sewage down my Polar Dawn walls!

And the grey ones? When I shut the tap off, they clang and bang like Jacob Marley lives down there.

Open Up The Wall

Now I have to go down and check that nothing has sprung a leak above the electrical panel. I don't HAVE to ... but I have to ... what if the electrical panel gets wet and shorts out the whole electrical system, or electrocutes somebody? There are so many wires down there, swirling around the ceiling like so many species of deadly snakes. They come out of the panel in an orderly manner, but then quickly join up in groups of two or three and make a dash across the ceiling until they escape out of sight to the floors above. And then the furnace sucks in its deep breath and exhales hot air, sighing: "Smells Like Gas To Me..."

I just wanted to close the basement door and hope that nothing down there ever flooded or caught fire or blew up, but my mind was going full out with worst-case scenarios, all because I didn't know how any of it worked. I had spent my last dollar on this collection of wood, pipes, and wires and I was damned if I was going to let it rule me. This was my biggest asset, and I wanted to own it in every sense of the word.

But how to proceed? There was no Internet yet. No Google to keep dumb questions anonymous. No home reno shows on TV for encouragement. There was only the YELLOW PAGES.

If somebody needed a new toilet, they looked in the Yellow Pages under "Plumbing Contractors" because in those days the idea of spending a Saturday putting in a new toilet was as foreign a concept as NOT spanking children. A plumber plumbed and a baker baked and never the twain did meet.

However, the tide was beginning to turn and there seemed to be a growing interest in the Do-It-Yourselfer.

There were occasional articles about the hands-on homeowner in the weekend papers, giving me all the encouragement I needed to get my hands dirty. It was part genuine curiosity about how things worked, part cost saving, and part wanting to beat the Geoffrey out of me.

As a housewarming gift, I had been given The Reader's Digest Guide to Home Improvement, complete with pictures. This fat yellow book gave me a basic understanding of the material and the tools that I would need in order to fix my tap or insulate my basement. The pictures made everything look pretty simple.

"This looks pretty simple," I said to my wife, Dixie. "I think that I could move those pipes into the new bathroom myself."

"OK ... but why would you want to?"

"I don't know. Just to see if I can, I guess."

"That doesn't sound like you," she replied. "This is a side of you I don't know."

"Yeah, me neither."

Dixie was my first love. Even though we had been together for eight years by then, our horizons were still expanding, and we were still encouraging the best from each other. I knew that I could count on her to embrace this new endeavour of mine, and indeed, she waded right in.

We went through what we thought had to be done and, when it was clear that I could not cause the house to fall down just by adding on to the pipes that were already there, I began to get excited. Dixie measured and marked where the new tub was to go and I made a list of what I would need.

Then came the point where there was nothing more

Open Up The Wall

to talk about. I heard myself say: "Guess I'll go get some copper pipe and get started."

"OK. Good luck!"

Luck — when preparation meets opportunity.

I was lacking the preparation part, so by the time I had accumulated everything I needed for the job, I had made four trips to the Building Supply Centre. On each trip I had self-doubt creeping around my ear, disguising itself as logic.

"You sure you want to go through with this? If you screw this up it will be double the work to fix it."

"Why are you doing this to yourself? There are so many other things that you should be doing. Call a plumber before it's too late!!"

On my final trip to get special sandpaper to sand copper pipe with (!?!) I revisited a childhood memory of when I was about ten — finally old enough to dive off the high diving board at the Civic Centre. One cloudy Saturday afternoon, I saw a middle-aged man in striped swim trunks climb the ladder to the high diving board. He walked to the end of the board and looked down at the water below him. After a few seconds he gingerly turned and climbed back down the ladder. Even at ten years old, I thought less of the man. The dive is always worth it.

Down at the Building Supply Centre – aka 'The Lumber Yard' – I knew that I didn't fit in. My clothes had no rips or paint spatter to identify me as having a right to be in this place. I wore shoes, not work boots with the toes worn down to the steel, and I probably looked nervous lined up with the pros at the order desk.

The order desk that behaved like a bar. It was a length

of unpainted plywood, and every square inch of it was covered in the pen and pencil legacy of career tradesmen. There were lists of numbers and fractions, phone numbers, a drawing of the bird's eye view of a bathroom, drawings of baseboard profiles. There was a beautiful drawing of a running horse, a not so beautiful naked woman with breasts of different sizes, and a drawing of a ruler. In between inch 1 and 2 were the letters 'CH'. I was told that a CH is one of the oldest measurements in history. It describes an almost imperceptible length, a measure so very tiny that a carpenter would say, "... cut me a piece of wood just a CH over 65¼." CH means Cunt Hair. The term is still used a bit, but has mostly found its place in carpentry history, replaced by the politically correct measurements of "fat" or "thin." So nowadays "a Cunt Hair over 65¼" becomes "65 and a fat ¼."

Behind the bar were the knowledgeable and surly staff. We took a number, and waited to hear "Alright, who's next?" The holder of the number would place his order, go to the cashier and pay up, take two copies of the receipt and head to The Yard, where a surly yardman would load the order into your truck ... if you had a truck. If you had a subcompact sedan with a roof rack, like I did, they got extra surly.

This was the prevailing attitude toward 'civilians', as we interlopers were called. We were the time wasters, asking questions like "What would you recommend?" We hemmed and hawed while they tapped their pens. Trucks and vans idled in line while the civilians at the front tied drywall to their roof racks with string. We were the wrench in the works of the streamlined

Open Up The Wall

operation of getting tradesmen loaded up and off to a jobsite as quickly as possible.

I leaned on the order desk as I had seen the pros do, and waited my turn.

Ponytail Jim behind the counter looked me up and down. "What are you tearing at?" he asked.

"Sorry, what?"

"What are you tearing at? What's your project?"

"Oh. I'm putting an old clawfoot bathtub in my new bathroom ... just moving things around a bit."

In the film *Lawrence of Arabia*, Peter O'Toole tells Omar Sharif that he intends to walk across the deadly Nefud desert to Akaba, and Omar Sharif laughs at the absurd naivety of the plan.

Ponytail Jim now laughed that same laugh at me. I noticed his missing teeth.

"I got the pipes already ..."

"I know. I seen you in here a couple a times today."

"Well, I'm figuring things out as I go, so I need that paste stuff that you put on pipes before you heat them."

"Yeah – flux. Anything else?"

"Um ..."

"You need a brush to apply flux."

"Oh. Yes. And a brush please."

"Anything else?"

"Um, no?"

In The Guide to Home Improvement the pictures of plumbing were pretty straightforward. The drain part looked simple. It is plastic, so it gets put together like Lego. The copper part involves heating the connections with a propane torch and putting solder in the joints.

This troubled me, and my imagination was no help.

Little films were running through my head where I would solder the connections badly and they would break apart in the middle of the night and water would pour down onto a light and cause a short in the electrical system and burn the house down.

Or water would pour onto the furnace and extinguish the pilot light and gas would fill the house and kill us in our sleep.

Or only a little water would seep out and leave an invisible slick at the bottom of the stairs and the first person down the stairs in the morning would slip on the slick, smack their head on the sideboard, break their neck and die.

Throughout the planning stages of this undertaking, these doomsday scenarios would visit me until finally I came to accept them as a strange kind of memento mori – benevolent death omens that would save our lives one day.

Very carefully, I got to work on the plumbing: Heat the pipe until the flame turns green, remove the flame, and quickly touch the solder to the hot copper. The solder sucks into the joints like magic. Simple. Fascinating to watch. I repeated this process with three connections:

Heat the pipe. Remove the flame. Touch the solder to the copper.

On the final connection I smelled smoke and turned to see the vanity door on fire! I reached up and turned on the tap, forgetting that I had dutifully followed Step 1 in the plumbing chapter: Be sure to turn water off at source!

Frantically, I wrapped the flaming door in a bath towel

Open Up The Wall

and, pulling it from its hinges, I threw the smoldering thing out the window into the yard below.

Heat the pipe. Remove the flame. Touch the solder to the copper.

AND WHEN YOU REMOVE THE FLAME, DON'T AIM IT AT YOUR VANITY DOOR!!

This definitely counted as "Not Being Good With My Hands." I fought back the disparaging voices in my head and moved on to hooking up the drain line.

Measure, test fit, glue together. Kind of like Lego. No problems putting in the drains. I was done. The bathtub looked good in its new spot, and the smoke was clearing nicely.

I called down to Dixie: "OK, I'm done! But I have to make sure that I did the soldering properly and there are no leaks!"

"Leaks? Are you serious? What are the chances?"

"There is a good chance. I'm new at this. Go down to the basement and turn the tap on very slowly, but if I shout OFF! turn the tap off really quickly!"

I had a bucket and every last one of our towels standing by.

"OK! TURN ON THE TAP!"

From the basement I heard, "Oh please God ..."

The water hissed into the pipes. I couldn't see any leaks, and I couldn't hear any water hitting the floor.

"Do I turn the tap off?"

"NO, IT'S ALL GOOD! C'MON UP!"

I smelled like smoke, so I got the first bath. Lowering myself in gingerly, I realized that I was expecting something to go wrong. Nothing did, so I lay back in the tub and allowed myself to feel good for fifteen minutes, until I hopped out of the tub, pulled the plug, and turned to

the vanity with a missing door and prepared to shave.
 In the mirror I could see the tub behind me, still full of water. I could also see the plug resting on the side of the tub.
 The Guide to Home Improvement had a troubleshooting section. There was nothing in there about plugged bathtub drains, so I went back to the plumbing section. In the drain chapter, there was a picture of a level perched on a drainpipe. The caption read SLOPE. I didn't own a level but, now that it had been brought to my attention, I didn't need one to see that a section of my new drainpipe was sloping the wrong way. It was going uphill.
 When Ponytail Jim saw me come to the order desk, his grin was so wide I could see he was missing a molar.
 "You here for a level?"
 "What!? Yes. How did you know?"
 "No offence, but I saw it coming. It's a common mistake. Well, not that common. Anyway, do you have a hacksaw?"
 "A hacksaw?"
 "You're gonna have to cut out the drain pipe where you fucked up, aren't you?"
 "Ah, yes... which one would you recommend?"
 I took comfort in one phrase that I saw in my home improvement book. It described all of my mistakes and corrections as 'Sweat Equity'. Even though I beat myself up for having to redo my bathtub drain, the entire project had cost me less than $200, not including a new vanity door.
 I couldn't put a price on the thrill of playing plumber, and of working with my hands. Each step of the way there had been a special kind of satisfaction at putting something together. It was like spending the

Open Up The Wall 27

whole day doing one perfect parallel park after another.
   In order to bring the pipes to the bathtub's new location, I had to cut away some of the drywall ceiling below, so now this had to be replaced. Dixie helped me lift the drywall onto the car roof while the surly yardman stared at her breasts. We loaded it into the house, patched the holes and painted it white.
   Next I figured out how to run wire upstairs so that I could install this innovative new product called a Trac light.
   Then I put a deck on the back of the house.
   Then I put lights in the attic.
   Then I insulated the attic.
   Then we sold the house.
   Then we bought a bigger fixer-upper, and I started the process all over again. For the sheer fun of it.
   My tool collection grew with each undertaking and so did my confidence – as well as my curiosity and my wonder. Electric power surging into my house became more mystical than just flicking a switch. I began to notice the many different sounds that water made, coming and going from my home. I wondered why there were so many types of insulation, and why some door slams sounded more solid than others. I stopped thinking about getting a sailboat, or living in Paris for a year, fantasizing instead about building a solar-powered log home.
   As my learning curve curved, I made plenty of mistakes, wasting time and money, but for the most part I didn't hold this against myself, taking inspiration from a little clipping that was taped on our fridge:
   Success comes from good judgment. Good judgment

comes from experience. Experience comes from bad judgment.

I was closing in on the 'experience' stage. There were things that I was doing for the second time, like putting up a ceiling fan. I was even helping my neighbours with minor repairs, because the word was out that Geoffrey was HANDY!

One spring morning, my neighbour Margaret came through the gate. She had a small gardening/landscaping company.

"Nice fence," she said. "Could you build one for a client of mine? You have to give the lady a price, and if she likes the price, she will pay you after the job is done. That's the way she wants it. Do you want to do it?"

"She'll pay me to build a fence? Hell yes! I sure do!"

Three: Stiffed

The renovation business seems to attract an above-average number of creative people. I have worked with actors, musicians, sculptors and filmmakers who consider their life in the trades an extension of their creative process. Taking jobs doing carpentry, tiling and painting is how they avoid being starving artists. Their creative process is such a part of their vitality that they shun mind-numbing jobs as waiters or night watchmen in favour of project work, where their contribution, no matter how small, is there for all to see at the end of the day. They also get to be themselves, because singing or reciting audition monologues is all tolerated on the jobsites that I have worked on. I have gone out at night to see plays, exhibits and bands at the invitation of the artist, whom I have worked with during the day.

Stan was an actor I had known by reputation for a number of years. His height and his muscular build made him a natural as the 'Bad Guy', but he had wicked comic timing, so his bad guy roles were usually in a comedy. I finally met him when we were both cast in the same movie. I was surprised to learn that he was doing renovation work between acting gigs, and it soon became clear that Stan was way out of my league. He could do everything — plumbing, wiring, tiling — everything. Eventually Stan went into construction full-time, even building houses. Now there was something that I couldn't imagine Geoffrey ever doing.

Stan was a warm, witty guy and we had a lot of laughs whenever we met up at an audition. I would tell him about my little projects and he was always generous with a word of advice, which always ended up saving me a bit of time and money.

I saw him at the mall in the afternoon, and I told him my news, "My neighbour has a gardening business and she needs a fence built for one of her clients and she asked me if I would do it. I'm going over tonight to give her a quote."

He was not as impressed as I would have liked, but he wished me well and said "Get everything in writing."

I was in the mall to buy a professional-looking binder — the steel ones that all the contractors carry. I also needed the fine-tipped pens that all the contractors do their drawings with. I wanted to present as professional an image as I could for my meeting that evening. I had decided not to shave, but I was going to wear nice socks in case the client invited me indoors and I had to take my work boots off. Nothing was to be left to chance. I was nervous about building for a total stranger. Who wouldn't be?

At the appointed hour, with pens, binder and tape measure in hand, I knocked on the door. A small man with a large beard opened the door. He said nothing.

"Good evening," I said. "My name is Geoff. I have been asked to provide a price for a new fence."

"You want Inga. She's out back. Go between the houses."

The little man had his mouth open, as if to speak. I waited, but he just kept staring at me. Finally, he closed the door in my face.

Open Up The Wall

I went around the back.

"You must be Geoffrey. Dave told me you were here. I'm Inga."

"Pleased to meet you," I replied, "and call me Geoff."

Inga was a large woman with a tight, severe mouth. Her grey hair was dirty and her yard was a mess. I couldn't tell if she was avoiding eye contact or just keeping her eyes on the fence.

"I can't afford anything fancy, just your basic fence, high enough so I don't have to deal with my awful neighbours."

"OK, so a straight board fence?"

"Oh God no! It's gotta look pretty. I want a fence made out of lattice."

"Well, that will look pretty, but it won't afford you as much privacy."

Inga flashed a look like she was going to kill me, but covered it in an instant. She smiled and said, "It's going to be lattice. How much?"

"Lattice it is," I said. "I'll take some measurements and get back to you."

"Thank you, Geoffrey. C'mon, Dave."

The little man with the beard was standing at the corner of the house looking for all the world like a garden gnome. With his eyes on the ground, he edged past me and followed Inga into the house.

I had a different tone at the order desk this time.

"Awright, who's next?"

"That's me. Yeah, the lady wants a lattice fence." And then I kind of rolled my eyes the way I had observed other contractors doing. It said, "It's not my idea, but what can I do?" Then I placed my order and said "Have a good one," the way all the other guys did.

I would have liked to have told him that this was my first professional job, that I was a bit nervous about building a fence for pay, but that would have got me laughed out of the place.

The fence was only twenty feet long, so after digging the postholes four feet down and pouring the concrete piers, I had it built in two days. When I was done I took a lot of pictures from a lot of angles. This fence was identical to the one I had put up at my own house but I was more proud of my work on this one, because getting paid for a job made it more real. I was a PROFESSIONAL. Oh, if my mother could see me now — Geoffrey hired to do manual labour. Oh dear...

I had bought a book of invoices with duplicate copies and wrote up my first invoice. As instructed, I left it in Inga's mailbox for her bookkeeper to pick up.

After twelve days I called Inga. I got her answering machine.

Two days after that, I left another message. I called again the next day, and Inga answered. She said that she had given the invoice to her bookkeeper, and she would see to it that a cheque was delivered to my house that evening.

Two days after that, I knocked on her door. Dave opened it. He let me in and scurried off. Inga came down the stairs and said, "You're here about that so-called invoice. Well, I don't know where to begin."

"What's the problem with it?" I asked. "It couldn't be more straightforward."

"Yeah? Says you! You call that a fence? It's all crooked!"

I was not used to being talked to in this way — ever —

Open Up The Wall

and it made me mad. I tried to stay businesslike.

"Where is it crooked? Show me."

"I don't mean crooked ... I mean the lattice is on wrong. "

"How is that possible?"

"You put the lattice in vertically! It's supposed to be horizontal!!"

I had to think about that for a second.

"That's crazy! The lattice is square. There is no vertical or horizontal."

"Yeah? Says you! You took the lazy man's way out, and you ruined my fence! I'm certainly not paying for such shoddy work. I'll pay you for the material and that's all, because now I'm gonna have to pay someone else to fix your shoddy work!!!"

She was yelling a shrill, grating yell. Dave stood to my right with his arms folded across his chest.

I said, "Inga, your fence looks great. It is solid. It's square. If you are having trouble paying the full amount right now, we can work something out, but you have to pay me."

"How dare you talk down to me! Get out! Dave! Get him out!"

Dave moved menacingly closer. The thought of the little gnome trying to push me out the door made me laugh, which was how I made my exit — laughing.

I cried on the way home. Inwardly of course. I was going to call my shrink, but I called Stan instead.

"I could use some advice," I said. "I built the fence, but the woman won't pay me."

"Did she give you a good reason, or a bullshit reason?"

"She says I put square lattice on vertically, but she

wants it horizontally."

"A bullshit reason, which means that she never had any intention of paying you. How much did she stiff you for?"

"About $450."

"Not so bad. Well, you have to take her to small claims court. It's quite a process, and they never give the tradesman the full amount, but you have to do it."

"It hardly sounds worth the effort for $450."

"You're not going for the money! You're going for your reputation! Look, did you do a good job on the fence?"

"Yes."

"Did you do it to code?"

"Yes."

"Then why would you give this woman a free fence? If you don't go to court, she will be talking about you and her free fence. But if you take her to court, she won't say a word to anyone."

"Jesus, of course! She'll be talking about me!"

"Nip this in the bud. In this business, all you have is your tools and your reputation. Keep them both clean!"

"Wow ... well said. Do you want to come to court with me?"

"What? No!"

I paid a paralegal to serve the summons on the woman, then I took a lawyer friend to lunch and got tips on what to do in a court and how to impress a judge. By the time I got to pre-trial, I had spent about $120 on my $454.70 complaint. Pre-trial is where both parties sit across from each other, while a mediator encourages a settlement.

Open Up The Wall

It looked as though Inga hadn't washed her hair since I saw her last. She sat with downcast eyes and heavy brown eye shadow. She spoke against me and my fence, citing shoddy workmanship. She was vague in her examples, and picked at her brown nail polish with short stabbing pecks.

Staring across at her after four months, I felt my anger rising all over again and I caught the mediator looking at my clenched fists. I was in danger of losing my focus and becoming inarticulate when it became my turn to speak, so in my mind I resolved to punish Inga further, some day, somewhere, regardless of the outcome of this case. Having a malevolent plan helped me to calm down.

I made a point of reminding her about the lattice going in vertically, not horizontally, knowing that she would sound really stupid trying to explain that one. And she did. She sounded ridiculous. Then I showed pictures of the work to Mr. Mediator, and he said it looked fine to him. "Of a professional standard" were his words. He suggested that she pay me $300. She said that she couldn't afford that much. I asked her if she had ever had enough money to pay for a new fence. She told me to mind my own business. The mediator laughed, and said that it was my business, and that's why we were here.

We settled on $175.

I had come to understand through this ludicrous process that, without a reputation, a tradesman would not move forward in the building business where ultimately, success depends on word of mouth. It was also easy to understand now how a miscommunication or a personality clash with a client would mean the end of my career before it had even got off the ground. I imagined some vengeful soul getting on Facebook and badmouthing me, and I could picture the comments:

"Thanks for the warning. I'll be sure to never use him!"

Luckily, I had no clients. My reputation at this point was limited to Stan, so it was especially important that I tell him that I had won, and that the mediator said I had done a professional job on the fence.

"Well, congratulations," he said.

Then ... this is what I heard him say next:

"I may have some work for you, if you're interested."

Four: The New World

I had to make sure.
"You mean you're offering me a job?"
"Indirectly, but yes. I'm working for my friend Greg and he's building a full-service recording facility — two studios, two control rooms, four offices and a lounge. There's a lot of drywall to go up, so he needs more guys. I told him that you had some skills, so he said to bring you along and we'll see how you work out."

The timing couldn't have been better, because I was in the midst of a career crisis. For the past twenty-five years, I had been making a very good living as an actor. I was well known in the industry, and I had won awards, but my heart just wasn't in it anymore. I was forty-five years old and I didn't like the roles that I was getting, now that I was not young but not old. However, the business had been lucrative. I owned three houses now, and fixing them up had become my preferred creative outlet.

I loved working in the theatre and I love actors, but I had two kids now, and it was painful leaving them to spend ten weeks in a theatre on the other side of the country. Dixie began to get leading roles at a summer Shakespearean festival, so we pulled the kids out of school and relocated to the festival town every March, and returned home every October. The older they got, the harder this was on them, so we had made the decision to stay put. I suppose that was when I began to make career choices based on the salary, and I suppose that was when I became bitter.

We had only one rule: Do not look stupid on National TV. For this reason, we stopped doing commercials, relying instead on episodic TV shows, and movies-of-the-week to pay the bills. I hit Mr .T with a barbell, I injected Robert Urich with a toxic serum, I threatened James Woods with financial ruin, I begged Tom Sizemore to spare me from financial ruin, I delivered Farrah Fawcett's baby, I turned a whole town against Yasmine Bleeth, I left John Corbett in a hole. I betrayed Bruce Dern, I gunned down lots of people, and I got gunned down a lot. I simulated sex and I made racial slurs.

My little boy once saw some show in which I was executed with a bullet to the back of the head. In his glorious four-year-old innocence, he couldn't separate the fantasy from the reality, and the shocking images made him cry. I had done a lot of shows that I wouldn't want my kids to see. I was in a business that was losing its appeal. Things hadn't gone the way that I imagined they would.

Stan asked, "Are you in?"

"Are you kidding? Yes!"

"Great. Next Monday, 8:00 a.m."

On Sunday night I double checked that my cordless drill was charged, I loaded new blades into my drywall knives, I vacuumed out my tool bag and, finally confident that I was completely prepared, went to bed. But I woke up worrying that the frayed lace on my boot would break and I would be embarrassed in front of seasoned pros. I was nervous because, while I pretty much knew what to expect putting up drywall, I didn't know what was expected of ME. I just didn't want to come off as a Geoffrey on my first day. I just wanted to fit in.

At 7:48 I walked onto the jobsite. Stan was already there and he showed me around. There were tool belts, tools, and

Open Up The Wall

hardhats neatly piled in various corners of the space, belonging to other workers. There was drywall piled neatly against most of the walls. The floors were swept clean and in the middle of the space were stacks of metal stud.

"Ever worked with metal stud before?" asked Stan.

"No."

"You'll like it. It's really light and you can cut it with tin shears, and it screws together with these little screws. Let's get on with it — you'll pick it up in no time."

And to my joy, I did. I wasn't as fast as Stan, but I didn't make any mistakes as we put up a large wall. Other guys came in and I was introduced casually:

"This is Geoff."

"Hey."

"This is Geoff."

"Dude!"

Stan, I guess, felt comfortable leaving me alone to make stud walls.

"I'll be in the front studio if you need me. Greg will be here soon, so I'll send him back to see how you're getting along."

Ah yes ... a reminder that this was my tryout.

I measured, cut my studs, and pinched them together with thumb and forefinger while I screwed them into their top and bottom plates. I was doing fine, I had it down, and I was picking up speed.

I pinched the next two pieces of tin stud together, and screwed. This time though, my pinching finger was in the way and the screw bored through the stud and into my finger. Out came an involuntarily gasp of pain – "AAHH!" I quickly made like I was singing a Beatles song: "AAHH .... Look at all the lonely people..."

I got away with it. Nobody noticed. I was checking the damage, when I heard a voice behind me say:
"You must be a Geoffrey."
It was Greg ... and I hadn't heard him correctly.
He seemed very young to be the head of this million-dollar-plus undertaking, looking thirty-something, with a slim build and that kind of straight hair that doesn't respond to styling and just lay on his forehead. But his gaze was direct and his was voice was confident. I knew I was talking to the boss.
"Call me Geoff," I said.
I quickly wiped the blood off my finger before we shook hands.
He smiled a crooked smile and said, "Thanks for helping me out."
Despite the enormous scope of the project, Greg remained easy going and, with me, very patient.
"I've got meetings with the clients and the sound engineer in here today," he continued, "so I want to give you an idea of what's going on so you aren't bumbling around looking like an idiot while they're here. Let's take a walk."
Greg led me down a hallway past stacks of drywall. A single bulb was the only light. We went through a steel frame doorway into a crooked room with a low ceiling.
"The front of this recording booth measures 9'11" wide, and the back measures 8'7" wide. All recording booths are built crooked — front to back, side to side, top to bottom. This is done so that sound won't bounce around like a billiard ball on a rectangular table. The irregularity of the shape dissipates the sound waves. So you're going to build me another one of these crooked boxes out of steel studs, and after that they need to be sound-proofed, then a

Open Up The Wall

41

couple of layers of drywall, and then we can start prettying them up. Cool?"

"I get that a crooked room will dissipate sound waves," I said, "but why do you want to do that?"

"To create dead air. The microphones are in there to pick up vocals and nothing else, not even room tone."

"You mean an empty room has a tone?"

"Not when I'm done with it, it won't!"

Looking down at my cordless drill, he laughed.

"That's not gonna last long."

By lunchtime, the concrete floor was covered in chunks of drywall and pieces of metal stud. The air was dusty. I had none of the anxiety about making a mess that I did working on my own home. Nobody was going to complain here! Just kick the junk out of the way and keep on working. This was a CONSTRUCTION SITE! GEOFFREY was on a construction site, WORKING WITH HIS HANDS. Oh if my family could see me now.

We left the building and went for lunch at the kind of place that doesn't mind serving tradesmen. Not like those gourmet coffee places, where guys in work boots are made to suffer the tsks and glares from stay-at-home moms as they weave their way through the aisles clogged with strollers. The staff would never go as far as to say "We don't want your kind coming here," but the terse and abrupt "Yes? Can I help you?" says the same thing. There is a reason why you don't see workers taking coffee breaks in those places. It's because of all the baristas with man buns and tattoo sleeves who treat them with disdain. Just because a man works with tools and gets his hands dirty doesn't mean that he isn't capable of having his feelings hurt.

Ironically, we went to The Patrician Grill.

These were early days on this enormous project, so the lunchtime talk was mostly Greg and Stan planning and troubleshooting. I just listened, extremely happy to even be there.

"We should finish the framing this week."

"Yeah, but there are two split beams holding up the stairs, so we will have to sister them up before we can frame the lobby."

"Somebody will have to lag 2X12s onto them."

"Ok, but can we still finish the back studio framing this week?"

"Geoff?"

I looked up from my soup. They were both looking at me.

Greg said: "Geoff, can you get the rest of the stud up in three days?"

"I don't know ... I guess... probably ..."

I saw Stan look away.

Greg spoke firmly to me. "Geoff, I have to plan for when to bring in the electricians, so I'm looking for a yes or no answer."

I hadn't given any thought to my place in the grand scheme of things. I had come with no idea of the big picture, no sense of responsibility for my part in this project, or the fact that I was being paid to help keep Greg's business running smoothly.

Greg was the 'G.C.' — the General Contractor. More General than Contractor. He was leading a small army of plumbers, electricians, HVAC (Heating/Ventilation/Air Conditioning) fabricators, roofers, drywallers, and specialty trades — security, telephone, Internet, even a stained-glass maker. Each of these trades had to be co-ordinated with the one coming before and after.

"I have the hang of metal stud now," I said, hoping I sounded confident. "So yes, I will be done in three days."

"It's totally doable," agreed Stan. "Anyway, you have to work with me tomorrow on the split beams, so if that throws off your timing, I'll give you a hand on Friday."

"That's what I like to hear," Greg said. "Because, y' know, my brothers, it's all about people helping people."

We laughed at his delivery, but the sentiment was right on.

Late in the afternoon on my second day, I smelled smoke, and then my drill stopped working.

"Burned out the motor," said Mike.

"How is this possible? I just got it!!"

"Yeah? Where'd you get it? Toys R Us? C'mon, you can't expect that thing to screw metal for eight hours a day and live very long."

Yes I could! I expected tools to live a lifetime, not give out after a few months! Granted, I had always walked past the expensive tools that said 'HEAVY DUTY' on them and chosen the cheap one. The idea that a tool could be worn out simply by being used ... well, that was something that I would have to get used to. This was the first of my weekend handyman tools to go.

I could see that everyone else had the brands that cost a lot of money. I didn't want to spend $300 on a drill, but I had to get a lot of studs screwed together in the next three days and I couldn't afford any delays from another burned-out toy tool, so really, what choice does a worker have? It is understood that you will show up with your side arms — a tool belt, hammer, tape measure, pencils, blade (box cutter), speed square, AND a cordless drill and drill bits. Just to get in the game will cost you about $600. Pay starts at around $15 per hour.

That night, after work, I spent the $300 and got the drill that everybody else had. It felt good. It had a confident sounding motor, a sympathetic grip, and enough power in two batteries to work with me all day.

I had never before felt worthy of such a tool. In the back of my mind I was still expecting to fail at manual endeavour, so I reasoned that if the tools were cheap when I threw them all away in a fit of failure fury ... well, no great loss. This time, however, an expensive drill was an investment in my future.

I took a permanent marker and put my initials all over the drill, the batteries, and the case, just as everyone else had done with theirs. In the studio, there were identical drill cases lined up like homes in a subdivision. In lieu of house numbers there were decals, paint splatter, gouges, scratches, names, and initials. I initialed my drill as I signed my cheques. It looked a bit flowery on a drill, and I woke up anxious about my choice. I was anxious that the guys at work would see my swirly initials and they would ... what? Laugh at me? Ignore me? Sneak off to lunch without me? Beat me up? I didn't know ... I JUST WANTED TO FIT IN! I liked working there so much, I didn't want to be that worker that nobody relates to and is the first to get laid off — like the nice guy with bad breath.

All my anxiety went somewhere else when I got down to work with my new drill. I planned out where I had to get to each day if I was going to finish by Friday, so I had the focus that I needed to push anxiety out of

Open Up The Wall

my consciousness and in no time I found myself in 'the zone'.

Greg describes 'the zone' as the state of bliss where the worker, the tools, and the materials are one, and all energy is focused on the task at hand. In the zone, my drill was making her presence known. She felt smooth and balanced in my hand and, of course, performed much better than her plastic predecessor. Our relationship was off to a good start.

I woke up Friday morning with a great sense of purpose. Today I would finish framing the walls of a major recording studio in a major metropolis in North America, frequented by major recording artists. Today would be the last day for the lazy pile of metal studs that had been lolling on the floor all week. Today was the day that every last one of them would be yanked upright and put to work as a wall!

By lunchtime, the end was in sight. I was whistling, and wondering why. I never whistled before. I stopped when I saw Greg weaving his way through the studios towards me.

"Got some work for you up front," he called.

I followed him to the front, where the foyer/reception area would be.

"I want to get drywall up in here by the end of today. Make sure you cut out the window openings, so they can see all the way through to the back studio, OK?"

"But that will take all afternoon, and you said I have to finish framing today."

"Fuck the framing. I'll get someone to finish it later."

"I'm almost finished ..."

Greg sighed and pushed his flaxen hair back out of his eyes. "Listen, it's Friday, and on Friday it is more important to do something sexy for the clients to see than it is to finish the back wall!"

"What? What are you talking about?"

"It's like this. After work on Friday, the clients and their staff will come up here to see how their studios are coming along. They want to see progress."

"Well, the cable has been run, and there's lots more duct work ..."

I could see that Greg was getting impatient with me.

"Dude! That is not sexy progress! The accountants aren't going to go gaga over the cable connection. The receptionists don't care about your framing. At this point, they need to be getting a sense of their future workspace, so we are going to give them a few walls. When this space has definition, they will be able to imagine their future, like where to put the desk and the plants. That kind of thing."

"Something sexy?"

"It's not a fucking joke. At the end of the week you always leave the client with something they can see and understand. They can't read plans, so if they can see it for real off the page, and in their space, I avoid a lot of miscommunication."

"I got it. Very clever."

"And you sweep the hell out of this place so that when they walk in here with their spike heels, nobody slips on a drywall screw and sues me!"

Sure enough, at 5:00 p.m. in came the clients and their staff from the floor below:

"Oh wow, it's so much bigger than I imagined."

"Hey, we could fit a coat rack along here."

"Oh THIS is what you meant by a bulkhead! I couldn't picture it."

"Great job, Greg, it's really coming along!"

We workers repaired to the bar on the corner.

Open Up The Wall

On the way in, Stan handed me a folded cheque and said, "Here. Good week," and then pushed past me to the bar.

I unfolded my cheque. On the line beside his signature, Stan had written 'casual labour'.

A week long bombardment of sights, sounds, and smells that I had never encountered up close before had kept me anything but casual. 'Aiming to please labourer playing catch up' would have been more like it.

I stood aside, out of sight, just to look at my cheque for a moment. I didn't actually make a point of stopping to mark the moment like you would if you were quitting drinking or something. It was just a quick moment of reflection.

Sometimes when I see my dog lying at my feet, I will suddenly regard her anew, and marvel that I share my space with another species. So it was with this familiar/unfamiliar cheque. So it was when I walked towards the backs of my new co-workers sitting at the bar. Plaid shirts, hoodies, well-worn boots. It was all just too familiar/unfamiliar. I had seen these guys in bars my whole life. Now I was one of them.

The talk always returned to the job. The decompression time was longer than I was used to. A question got answered with a diagram on a coaster. Scheduling was re-worked constantly. When it was discovered that I was left-handed, there was a change of plan for the coming week. I was to help Stan put up 2X12 structural support beams. I would be hammering from the left.

There was an interesting bit of talk about women. I almost missed it. It went like this:

"Did anybody hear those two?" Mike called down the bar.

"What — 'sexy in a toolbelt'"? Asked Greg.

"Yeah, she was doing the toolbelt thing, but she was

making these noises like rushing water or a toilet flushing ... and then laughing with that other woman."

I had heard the weird noises.

"Wait," I said. "Do you mean that the woman in the suit was coming on to you?"

"Oh God. No." Greg laughed. "She didn't mean anything by it. You're gonna find out that there are a ton of women out there who think it's OK to talk dirty to guys in toolbelts."

"Seriously?" I asked. "Those office girls?"

"And stay-at-home moms and women who work from home. But they have to be in groups. They would never do it one to one, because then it wouldn't be a joke."

Mike said, "The other one was trying to make some kind of joke, but she couldn't stop laughing."

"Let them have their fun," said Greg. "It's all about people helping people." There was a lame laugh from us all, and then Greg turned his direct steely gaze on me and said: "NEVER joke back with a woman, ESPECIALLY if you are alone."

Five: Fitting In

Monday morning was cold, and there were roofers pouring tar and gravel on the flat roof. To keep warm, they hung around the fire escape door.
Smoking. Watching us. Watching our tools.
From the roof Greg called down to me: "You know what you're doing?"
"I have to finish in the back," I called back. "I've got twelve studs to screw together."
"HAHAHA," from the roofers.
"You don't screw studs, you screw chicks ... UNLESS YOU"RE A FAGGOT! HAHAHA"
"Hey those are steel studs! Careful you don't cut your dick off! HAHAHA."
"Which end is the ASS end OF A STUD? This guy needs to know THAT! HAHAHA."
I smiled and nodded like an idiot. Nobody in the world knows how to deal with such Neanderthal remarks from a total stranger.
Stan came ambling down the hall, dangling his framing hammer in his hand. It had an oversized iron head and a long wooden handle, looking for all the world like a medieval weapon. Stan stands about 6'3" so it looks normal on him.
"You guys are so funny," he said, towering over the motley crew. "I could just kiss each one of you!" Moving closer to the lead joker, he added: "After all, it's about people helping people, right?"

"Sure ... whatever dude ..." and they all backed up the fire escape to the roof.

Greg made his way back to me a few minutes later.

"Come here," he whispered.

"Why are you whispering?" I whispered.

"Because I don't want those fuckwits on the roof to hear us. Now listen — I don't trust them alone with our tools, and you're the new guy, so you are the one who has to stay here at lunch and guard our tools. Cool?"

"Sure," I whispered back, "but what should I do if I catch someone stealing something?"

"Kick the shit out of him."

!?!?!

At lunch, I had a look around to see where everybody had piled their gear. There were drill boxes, milk crates, tool bags, and grocery bags filled with battery chargers, sandpaper, extra blades, pencils, caulking guns — things that they had been bringing in as they were needed. This sea of gear was worth thousands of dollars.

I just had a tool bag, so I sat on it, ate some old Timbits and waited for the roofers to take lunch.

They came down from the roof with lots of "Fukkin Freezin's" and "Fukkin froze my nuts off's". They were cold and miserable but they were pleasant enough as they came in to the warmth. I felt sorry for their lot in life, and grateful for my birthright.

They all passed by and headed for the washroom to clean up. There was silence on my watch. Then there was the shuffling of feet.

I did not want to investigate this, but I knew that I had to. I got up and tiptoed around to where I could peek between the open walls. A head rose up from below the

Open Up The Wall

sheets of drywall. The body followed, and in one hand was a hammer. I stomped around the corner and brought myself face to face with the roofer. Then I said:
"Put it back!"
His eyes told me that he was lying when he said:
"I was just lookin' at it."
"Put it back, you cock!"
"What? Umm ... No worries Bro, but did you just call me a cock?"
"Just put the fucking hammer back!"
The thief never stopped smiling. He deliberately dropped the hammer far from where he picked it up.
"There," he said. "Happy?" He walked away.
From the washroom I heard, "What? A cock?" "HAHAHA!" "Put it back, you cock!" "HAHAHA!" "Fucking faggot!"
Chevy Chase made a career out of being a weak, hapless boob and, to me, he was a deeply embarrassing character. You could have written my performance with the roofer into any one of his National Lampoon movies. Why would I EVER say such a weak and ineffectual thing as "Put it back, you cock"?
I was full on feeling like a Geoffrey by the time everybody came back from lunch.
"We got you a BLT. What's happening?"
They were livid at my news. Each one checked their tools. As I had been the security detail, I was relieved that nothing else was missing.
"Which one was it?" Greg asked.
"The guy with the neck tattoo."
Mike was the quiet one on the crew. Now he punched the wall and said: "Nothing is lower than

stealing a man's tools. One trade stealing from another? I'm going to fucking kill those guys."

Greg shot up from his seat on the floor and shouted "HEY!"

We all froze, it was so startling.

"Whatever happens next has to be one on one," he cautioned. "I don't want a fucking brawl in here. Geoff — when you caught the prick what did you do?"

"I told him to put it back. He dropped it and left."

"You didn't threaten him, or inflame the situation?"

"All I said was, 'Put it back, you cock'."

"...You called him a cock?"

"I ... I have never said that before, never called anyone a cock before ..."

"Well, no, not on its own like that. Cocksucker maybe, but..."

The roofers were gone the next day but the incident had changed the working dynamic around the place. There was a more protective attitude towards leaving valuable tools lying around. Tools that were not being used for a few days were now being taken back to their vans and locked up. The electrical crew had big rolls of copper wire worth hundreds of dollars. They took to chaining them up at night.

Stan explained to me that this was not a trust issue within our crew.

"We work together, we rely on each other and we definitely trust each other. But we have all — including you — been getting lax about leaving stuff lying around for the taking. There are new trades coming in every day, there's a cleaning staff, a floor full of people below. You get the picture?"

Open Up The Wall

"Yes."

"Here's the thing: everybody has a story about getting tools stolen, and there is one thread running through all the stories. They all talk about mistrusting everyone around them, including people they have worked with for years. That's a situation you don't ever want to be around. It will poison a working environment and bring bad blood to a job site."

Greg came over.

"What are you guys talking about?"

"Theft."

"Yeah, that was close. It's taken me about ten years to get a good group of subtrades that I can trust, but my regular roofers are residential roofers, so they don't do industrial jobs. This company has a good rep, so I gave them a try. Live and learn. What can I say, nobody died. Now get back to work."

Even with my eyes closed, I could hear and feel the rhythm for that day. First, the metallic whirr of a tape measure being pulled out, then the snap of the tape retracting after the measurement is taken. Then the steady plod/scuff of a work boot walking to a pile of drywall. The hiss of a blade slicing the drywall and the crack as the drywall is split to size. Another plod/scuff walk, then the ubiquitous oath: either "Fuckin' A" if the drywall fits or just "Fuck" if it doesn't. Finally the meow of a cordless drill as the drywall screws are fastened. Then the whole thing over again, and again, a mesmerizing steady rhythm that moves a whole jobsite into 'The Zone'.

There is a special kind of focus required for repetitive physical tasks, one which doesn't allow the mind to wander or worry. For the first time in my working life, there was no inner monologue going on inside my head. There were numbers, and economy of movement: 98X36. Mutter the numbers all the way to the drywall stack, measure, cut, carry the sheet to the studs, screw. Next – 36X9¼ ... and do it all again, and again, until there was a wall.

"Did I put the garbage out?" "What did she mean by...." All these thoughts would have to wait until the studs were covered in drywall, the meditation ended, and I could say a meaningful "Fucking A" and end the day, happy with my work.

Before Vincent Van Gogh ever picked up a paintbrush, he had embarked on a number of careers — working as a school teacher in Epsom, as an antique book dealer in London, and as an evangelical preacher in Belgian coal mines, before discovering his true calling in his late twenties. I was getting a feeling that I might have stumbled on my true calling. I felt at home in this dusty maze of crooked rooms. I was free from political correctness, diplomacy, and obligatory pleasantries. I trusted that anybody here would speak plainly to me if they were unhappy with what I was doing. I liked the people I was working with and I was proud to be part of such a fascinating and creative crew, even if I was just building walls. Sometimes I still couldn't believe that it was me standing alongside those skilled tradesmen, those guys that are so intimidating to so many anxious homeowners.

The stacks of drywall finally found themselves cut up and screwed onto the studio walls.

"You're done, Geoff," said Greg. "Pretty good work. I like your enthusiasm. Thanks."

"I ... I ... you mean you're firing me?"

"No! I'm not firing you! There's no more work for you, so I don't need you."

Open Up The Wall

"What about the doors, or the baseboards? I can do baseboards and trim."

"You don't have the skills, and you're too slow. I have a whole different crew coming in to do the finish carpentry."

"I understand. Well, this has been a fantastic experience, Greg, and I thank you for all that you've taught me."

"Right on. Keep in touch."

His phone rang and he went away.

I began to gather up my tools. I had purchased a lot of things for this job, just to keep up. I got a two-step ladder to reach the nine-foot ceilings. I got a jigsaw because it was too embarrassing always borrowing one. I got drywall blades and knives, kneepads, a four-foot level, a combination square, and a bigger tool bag. I was wondering if I would ever use them again.

To my horror, I started to tear up. I was acting like this was my last day at summer camp! I could NOT be seen like this, so when Mike walked by I said, "Damn! Something in my eye!" and quickly went down the fire escape to the truck with my first load of tools.

I had to pull myself together! Being my last day, the guys would probably want to take me for a beer. I had to be cool for that!

But they didn't. The Last Day was just another day for these men. When they left one job, they usually went straight to another one.

I just went home.

Six: Homework

I spent the remainder of the week fixing an area in my basement to hold all my new tools. I made dinners. I called my agent. Ho hum.

On Monday morning, I was on my way to get a haircut. I needed some money coming in, so I thought that if I got well groomed again, I could pick up a couple of days acting as a generic doctor/lawyer/politician.

Then Greg called.

"Need you to dig a few holes. You in?"

"Sure."

He gave me an address and we met there at the end of the day.

It was a nondescript wood-frame house. But behind the house was another building — a two-storey brick warehouse that had been used as an ice house at the turn of the century. Great blocks of ice had been stored in sawdust on the second floor. They would be loaded onto horse-drawn ice wagons, and delivered to the iceboxes in the area. This now-derelict eyesore was to be turned into an expensive dwelling.

"The building inspector wants to be sure that there is enough of a footing to make this place structurally sound, so I want you to dig down the side of the brick wall until you come to the bottom," Greg explained. "That's where you'll hit the footing. It is a wide slab of concrete that the brick wall rests on. Dig around it so we can see if it's thick enough and wide enough to hold this place up."

Open Up The Wall

"I'll start in the morning," I said.

"That should be enough time. The inspector will show up after lunch."

At 7:00 a.m., I started to dig down through a hard-packed mix of sand, stones, and tar. At about one foot deep I found a leather strap belonging to a horse's harness, and not far away were four small blue bottles for horse liniment. I dug further, with romantic visions of Old Dobbin, the dearest horse in the ice house, getting a rubdown at the end of a long day by a loving stable lass. I collected the harness, the bottles, a couple of horseshoes, and another bottle — this one was 'Sambo' rum. The logo was a drawing of a black man with disproportionally huge lips. The date on the back was 1922.

Digging this hole was like digging through time, and I let my mind wander off with fantasies of ice men and their horses, and their love, working together. It would be impossible to grow tired of a job where your partner was a horse.

At around the four-foot mark, I found a sack with three small raccoon skeletons in it. The next three feet were undisturbed sand, and in no time, there was a thunk, and I hit the footing. I exposed the concrete and then I shaved the sides of my hole so that it was wide enough for the building inspector to comfortably see the base of the footing. Now it was an attractive square pit.

The pit was about six feet deep. The sandy soil had made for such easy digging that my last break had been at the four-foot mark, when it had been easy to climb out. Now, two feet lower, I was stuck in the bottom of my hole. How to get out? The obvious solution was to notch myself some footholds in the walls, but when I stepped into them the sandy soil gave way under my weight.

It was getting to the point where I thought of

calling Dixie to come and pass down the ladder, which was lying at the top of the hole.

I was working on a plan to wedge my shovel in the firmer soil at the halfway point, and then climb on the handle to freedom, when I heard footsteps on the gravel outside. Two heads appeared at the top of my hole — Greg and the building inspector.

Holding his hair off his forehead, Greg looked down and called, "How's it going? You down to the footing yet?"

"Yeah, it's all exposed for you. Come down and take a look. You'll need the ladder though."

Down came the inspector and up went the Geoffrey. I'm pretty sure that neither of them clued in that I was trapped.

As things turned out, this minor event has had an impact on my life in construction.

I realized that I had not given enough thought to this hole, and to its purpose. I just brought a shovel and started digging. If I had thought things through, I would have brought not only a ladder, but also a bristle brush to scrub the walls and footings of loose dirt, a hatchet for chopping the roots out, a light to see by as the hole got deeper, a spade for squaring the walls, a garbage bag for all the debris that I had dug up, and some water for me.

I had come unprepared for the simplest of jobs. Had it been noticed, it would have put me in a class of worker only suited for general labour, the type never considered creative or even trustworthy. I decided on a plan: If I were to visualize myself doing the job in my mind — the whole process from start to finish — then surely I would see myself working with all the tools and

Open Up The Wall

material necessary for that particular project. With my mental virtual tour, nothing could be forgotten. Multi trips to the hardware store had become standard procedure for me when I worked on my own places, but it wouldn't cut it here, where time is money.

Minutes later, I had a chance to test my plan. Greg gave me another job putting up temporary lighting in the cavernous first floor. I visualized myself going through the whole process of running wire and connecting all the fixtures. It worked. It works to this day. The larger the project, the better it works.

Stan's van pulled up.

"Looks like I can use you up at the house," he said.

Greg's clients were staying in the apartment on the top half of the house while their ice house was being put together. The first floor was unlivable, thanks to the previous tenants, who kicked holes in the walls shorted out the kitchen wiring and, by the looks of things, never ever cleaned the bathroom. Greg had called in Stan to gut the entire floor, and renovate it. The three of us walked through the first floor, and Greg told us what he wanted:

"New kitchen, new bathroom, so all new plumbing and wiring, new front door, new bathroom door. Save the walls as best you can. Skin the floor with ¼" plywood and make it ready for carpet, or laminate ... they haven't decided. Oh yeah, it's a tile floor in the bathroom, and the tile should be here in a couple of days ... same with the light fixtures. The kitchen is all IKEA, so let me know when you want delivery. Sound good?"

"Sounds Good!" I crowed, noticing my overenthusiastic inflection. I was feeling the way I did doing volunteer work — useful.

Stan was still finishing at the studio, so I started on the

demolition. It's called demolition, but it is more like exploratory surgery, given the amount of precision cutting involved. Very little gets bashed down, compared to what gets cut away.

This is why God gave Man the Sawsall.

The technical name is reciprocating saw, but Sawsall says it all. It looks like a fish, a marlin, because at its nose is a long blade with the capability of slicing through whatever comes in its path. It doesn't whine or scream like most power tools, it growls. With a steady hand guiding it, the beast chews through wood, nails and pipe in the blink of an eye. It is another essential tool, costing me $175.

First up was to cut a 6" strip out of the walls, beside the light switches, from floor to ceiling. This would give the electricians their 'chase' — a space to run their new wire. The cut had to be exactly six inches wide all the way down, so that it could quickly be patched with a matching cut of drywall. Time is money.

At the ceiling, I could see that one of the floor joists above was pulling away from where it had been nailed in, eighty or one hundred years earlier. How many more were like that? If the joists on either side were in the same shape, the floor above could become a bit springy. Springy enough to crack the bathroom tile? Who's fault would that be? It was my call as I was doing the exploratory. What if there were ten bad joists? It would be an expensive job to cut away the ceiling and strengthen all the joists with joist hangers. What if I cut away the ceiling and they were all fine, except for one or two? What a waste of time and money! Probably better to leave things alone.

But what if that joist was the best one, and all the

Open Up The Wall

other nails in the ceiling were slowly and steadily working their way out? That would make things so bouncy on the second floor that not only would the tile crack, but a water pipe too!

What if a pipe split at the elbow just a bit and small steady drops of water landed on the toaster in the kitchen below ... and when the wife went to put down the toast, she got electrocuted by the water contact and when her husband came in and saw her slumped over the toaster and rushed to her aid but she was still in electrical contact so when he touched her, he fried too? When the kids came in and saw their dead fried parents, they would be scarred for life and get into drugs.

It was not worth the sleepless nights. I made a one-foot wide cut, the length of the ceiling, which gave me enough room to have a good look at the floor joists. Now I could see that somebody had switched the tub and the toilet location decades earlier. To get the new drainpipes in, they had cut out great chunks of three joists, rendering them incapable of support. My ghoulish imagination had saved the day. I cut the ceiling strip wider. Wide enough to get shoulders through is two feet. Room to work.

Then I moved on to the kitchen.

I turned off the water to the house and cut the water lines. Galvanized pipe. That's the grey pipe that brings water to the taps, and it corrodes over time. It has to be replaced with copper pipe, so I followed the galvanized to its source in the basement and carefully cut it off.

With the exploratory surgery part of the demo over, I took a crowbar and yanked the cabinets off the wall.

The other essential tool in construction is a pair of steel-toed boots. Obviously, they are for toe protection, but I quickly discovered that they were also an effective implement of destruction. I gave a cabinet door a kick. It broke off at the hinge and flew across the room, and I didn't feel a thing. So I kicked the countertop free of the cabinets. Then I kicked the doors off the cabinets, stomped all the drawers flat, and finally I kicked the cabinets apart. Now I stood in a pile of debris, thinking about a new show on TV called 'Holmes on Homes.'

The show has lots of money. They can afford to pay a junk removal company to haul away the onsite construction debris. This was a luxury that was scoffed at by a lot of renovators.

"If I put their junk removal costs into any of my quotes I'd never get a job."

Which is why I had kicked all the cabinetry flat. Now I could stack it all in my truck and take it to the dump. Even if it took four trips, it would still be half the cost of a junk removal company.

I heard footsteps on the stairs and a woman's voice said, "Oh my!"

I scrambled over the debris to the stairs. The client from the upstairs apartment was standing a few steps up.

"Sorry about the mess," I said. "I'll have it all out of here in an hour."

"I have no water."

"Aah ... well ... I turned it off ..."

"You could have told me."

"Oh dear, you're right. I'm so sorry, I wasn't thinking. I can have it on ...really soon. I just have to run out and get some pipe caps."

"I want to do laundry before dinner."

"Sure. I'm so sorry to put you out like this."

Open Up The Wall

"Just let me know when the water is back on," she said, and went back upstairs.

I hightailed it to the lumberyard to pick up end caps for the cut pipes and make things right with the woman. This particular lumberyard was a family owned business.

Two blocks from the lumberyard, I passed a parking lot with a sign — 'FUTURE SITE OF HOME DEPOT'.

"We got a couple of years before they're up and running, then we'll see," said Ronnie at the counter. "I figure all we gotta do is stay competitive. Money talks."

Ronnie's mother at the checkout wasn't so sure. "I don't think we're gonna make it," she said.

Seven: Know Your Place

I went back and capped the pipes. I turned the water on and went upstairs to make amends.

"The water is back on, with my apologies once again for my thoughtless oversight," I told the client. "I got caught up in my work and forgot all about the second floor."

"That's alright. Thank you," she said, and abruptly shut the door.

The woman had looked right through me. She didn't see me at all. She only saw a dusty workman who had screwed up her day.

I loaded all the junk into the truck. Then I swept up and vacuumed with Stans's mammoth industrial vac. I had to restore my status as a competent professional.

E.M Forster starts off his book Howard's End with two words that get a page to themselves — "Only Connect." The book is about the consequences of status, of not seeing a person for who they really are. I had missed making an initial connection with this woman, so she naturally formed the typical impression of the common worker.

Greg was there the next morning.

"BIG rule, dude. You have to tell them when you are going to turn off the water."

"Oh shit! She told you. Was she really pissed off?"

He pushed his hair off his face, keeping his hand on his head while he chastised me:

Open Up The Wall

"She was in the middle of doing laundry and the water stopped. What do you think? Look, this isn't commercial construction, where we have the place to ourselves. This is home renovation, as in somebody's HOME. If you act like an idiot, then I look like an idiot for hiring an idiot."

The woman, Gloria, came into the gutted kitchen.

"We picked out the tile, Greg. It's in the back of the Volvo. Could you get him to put it in the garage?"

The 'him' was me.

I accepted that I had lowered my own status to moron/helper for the duration of this job, and that it was entirely my own fault.

Richard and Eric, the electricians from the studio job, arrived.

"Hey! New guy! Good to see you again. What's your name again?"

"It's Geoff."

"Right, Jeff, sorry. How's it going?"

"Good. I got everything open for you."

"No, not quite. We'll be running wire across the ceilings in the living room and kitchen, so we will need 1/2" holes through the ceiling joists for the wire to go through."

My job was to make the electricians' job go quickly and easily. If they had to waste the morning cutting and drilling, their costs would increase substantially. You don't pay an electrician's hourly rate to do Joe jobs. That stuff gets left to the low-paid man on the crew. I cut another 6" strip out of the ceiling, and then drilled a hole in each joist, which were spaced every 16" down the length of the house.

"We're going to put in new switches and boxes," said Richard, "so you can take out all the old ones."

"The light switches are still in the switch boxes," I said. "Did you cut power to them?"

"Yes."

I unscrewed the switch from the box and pulled at the wires.

Richard went "BZZZT" and I jumped!

"Jesus! You scared me!" I said.

"My gift to you," replied Richard. "Always check that the power is off. Don't take anybody's word for it that you are safe. What's your name again?"

"Geoff."

"Jeff! Sorry. Damn! Why can't I remember that?"

My insignificance was overwhelming me today.

Just after lunch, Gloria came in. She held up a DVD cover of a kid's TV show, with my picture on it.

"Is this you?"

"Yes. I did that show a few years ago now ..."

"This is amazing! A movie star working on my house! Too amazing!"

Gloria asked a few of the standard questions – Ever met anybody famous? Are kissing scenes real?

Finally she said: "It's so dusty in here, I don't know how you can stand it. You should be in your mansion in Hollywood! Haha. Bye."

"Haha. Bye."

In this line of work, I had been mildly ashamed to be known as an actor, but at this moment the bit of recognition was timely. Maybe I needed a balance to working in construction. Time would tell.

"We're done ... uh ... buddy! See you on the next one."

Richard and Eric beat a hasty retreat and I swept up their mess. I was happy in my work.

Eight: Working Relationship

The walls and ceilings of old homes were made by nailing rough strips of wood, called lath, to the stud walls, and then covering them with plaster. The bonding agent was horsehair. I held a strip of lath in my hand, and broke off the chunk of plaster that had hardened around it some eighty years earlier. I let my imagination take me back a couple of generations to see a plasterer going to the city stables, where they kept the trolley horses. He would be wearing a long apron, as plasterers did, and he would have an empty sack that he would fill with horsehair. Then he would walk back to his jobsite, in his mind setting a target workload for the day for him and his apprentice, for this was a skilled trade. He would be adding horsehair to his plaster to get a mix so strong that it would not crack for centuries. He could never have foreseen the present renovation obsession, and he would be proud to see how hard it was to smash down his walls to make room for a bigger kitchen.

Now I was going to fill in these cracks and holes with a modern goo called Durabond 90. In the vernacular - mud.

As I expected, Stan was an expert at applying this mud. He taught me the ways to mix the powdered Durabond with water to get the right consistency for the different wall surfaces, sometimes as thick as cake batter and sometimes as thin as yogurt. He showed me how to use the various sizes of drywall blades to get an even finish, and the importance of keeping a clean blade by scraping the excess back onto the hock — the square palette that holds the mud after it has been mixed in the bucket.

There were just the two of us working. A far cry from the din of the studio, the working atmosphere here was calm, almost therapeutic. We each took a room and started mudding.

They say that if you want to get someone to talk, take them for a drive, as it is more comfortable opening up to someone while staring straight ahead, avoiding eye contact. The Catholics figured this out centuries ago and devised the confessional. Mudding in different rooms of the house served the same purpose.

"How do you know all this stuff, Stan? Plumbing, wiring, mudding. Did you go to school? Take courses?"

"No, I learned on the job. This is my ninth year doing this, so we could say that a lot of good stuff has rubbed off on me. I had good teachers."

"Who were they?"

"Contractors, renovators. I used to drive around looking for a jobsite — any jobsite — and then I would go in and ask if they needed any more hands. It worked out pretty well."

"You like it still?"

"I love the freedom."

The tinny clang of drywall blades slapping the hock, and then scraping the ceiling, put a calming rhythm in the air — a simple and relaxing metre, only broken when we kicked our stepladders into their next position."

"Why are you here?" Stan asked. "Why do you want to get into this?"

Open Up The Wall

"It appeals to something in me ..."

"Like what?"

"I haven't figured it all out yet, but one thing I really like is that there's nothing subjective about this kind of work," I said. "You can't judge my interpretation of drywall installation. It's either done right or it's wrong. It's an easier way to live."

"Yeah, for you, it's easy at this stage. At some point you will get a reputation, and if it is bad ... you won't work much. But if it's good, you will have to maintain it if you want to keep working. That is when it gets stressful. Reputation and word of mouth go hand in hand, and that's what keeps me in business. The pressure gets to me sometimes. Depends on the size and scope of the job."

"I'm surprised to hear that from you, Stan. You come across as so on top of everything."

"It's because I had alcoholic parents. What about you? Are you always insecure, or is it just to do with you starting up in construction?"

"I grew up that way. But wait — how has alcoholic parents made you such a take-charge-and-run-the-show kind of guy?"

"I couldn't rely on them for anything, so I had to take charge. I grew up looking after myself – getting breakfast, having a bath, things like that."

"Is that typical child of an alcoholic behaviour? Is it documented or anything? ... Stan ... you there?"

"I don't know ... it's what I think ..."

Sometimes the thoughts got finished, sometimes they didn't. The long silences were easy.

Stan came around the corner, looked at me and went back around the corner.

"What's with the noises?" he called out.

"What noises?"

"You make noises while you work. Disapproving noises."

"Oh ... yeah, I get frustrated. I should be better at this by now."

"Geoff, this isn't a pissing contest. You have some skills, and you have good instincts, so just show up every day, don't overthink and the rest will take care of itself."

We mixed our buckets and moved our ladders into new rooms. I wanted to say "Thanks for your trust in me, Stan" and "You're a good guy, Stan, I feel lucky to have run into you" but I couldn't yet.

"Where were we?" he called.

"I show up every day, and I'll be as good as you."

"No, before that. Why are you sort of nervous and insecure? Incest? Buggery?"

"Nothing so dramatic. It's garden variety lack of self-esteem. My shrink says it's because I was abandoned at birth."

"What the fuck? You're making that up!"

"I swear to God. My mom delivered me and took off for two years."

"That makes you more fucked up than me!"

I laughed. "I would never have imagined that construction workers talked about things like this."

"Yeah, well, on the one hand we've been trained to be emotionally vulnerable as actors, and on the other hand we've learned to give away nothing in order to keep the peace on a construction site. We're a strange hybrid you and me, and all the musicians, and sculptors and potters and painters who call this their day job."

Open Up The Wall

"This is where I want to be," I said.
"Then you ARE more fucked up than me."
There was a stack of steel beams in the middle of the ice house floor. Greg wanted them lifted the 12 feet up to the ceiling ... somehow. He wanted one steel beam on either side of the old wooden beams, and then bolted together with a foot-long bolt ... somehow. That part was entirely up to us.
"It has to be done by Friday," Greg said.
"Something sexy?" I asked.
"Something sexy."
"Danger pay?"
"Haha. Just be careful."
With a car jack and some chains, the steel beams got levered into position, but things got risky as the day wore on and our back and shoulder muscles fatigued. By the time we had pounded the beams into place temporarily, I could barely lift my short-handled sledgehammer.
Now we had to drill holes for the 12" bolts to go through, and then tighten the nuts. Greg had ordered the holes pre-drilled in the steel so all I had to do was aim my drill through the hole in the steel on one side, bore through the wooden beam, and come out through the hole in the steel on the other side. I watched Stan line up his drill with the holes and then mimicked his technique, moving on along the beam. I had about six holes to go when I hit the steel beam. The drill bit was moving at such high speed that when it hit the steel it came to an abrupt stop, with all of the drill rotation getting transferred to my wrist. The torque was so fierce that I was rotated clockwise off the ladder to the floor. My first thought was for my brand new drill. I had paid $120 for it and now it was hanging, smoking from

the beam, half drilled in. I climbed back up the ladder, put it in reverse, and began to back the bit out of the hole but I couldn't keep my grip on the drill and I had to let go. My forearm was burning, and my fingers wouldn't work.

I called to Stan. "Can you give me a hand? Literally?"

Stan backed my drill out of the beam and it was fine. My wrist was starting to swell. My mind was fighting feelings of being a Geoffrey and I knew I had to get back to work. I had been around long enough to observe that a sore wrist was no justification for not finishing the day. Stan finished the drilling while I pounded the bolts through the holes and tightened the nuts with my good hand.

"You have to get that checked out," said Stan. "Technically it's an 'industrial accident.' So at the end of the day we'll go to the clinic, they'll tape your wrist up, give you some paperwork for Greg. Then you'll need a fair bit of alcohol, and I know an awesome place."

We lined up behind kids with ear infections and runny noses and, when our turn came, the gorgeous nurse at the desk looked up at Stan and smiled.

"What brings you here today?" she asked.

"It's him," said Stan, putting his big arm around me. "He was abandoned at birth, and now he's sprained his wrist."

Nine: A Poor Choice

My truck was popular. All of the other guys had vans, which was where they kept their tools. If I kept my tools in the back of my truck, they would get stolen of course, so I had to unload and store my tools on site, which meant that my truck bed was usually empty, which meant that I was the guy who went and got stuff.

After we put the steel beams in place, we had to frame in new walls in the ice house. I went to get 2X6 lumber for the exterior walls and 2X4 lumber for the interior walls.

Drilling through the steel, I had not only sprained my wrist but I had also given my thumb a good bang, and now the nail was coming off. I stopped on my way to the lumber yard and picked up some Band-Aids.

There was a bad vibe at the lumber yard. The family was losing money, so they had cut their own salaries in half and their long-time employees were being let go one by one. Now there were 'Final Sale' posters above the sparsely stocked aisles. Ronnie and the other guy behind the order desk put on a brave face, but I could see defeat in their body language. It was getting uncomfortable to be in this place now.

I left the order desk and went to pay Ronnie's mother, the cashier.

She gave back my Visa card and said, "That's that. Good luck to you, dear."

I walked around the till and hugged her. She always smelled of peppermint.

"Oh," she said, "You're a sweetie. I don't know what I'm going to do without you guys coming around." She broke our embrace, looked in my eyes, said something in German and then made the sign of the cross.

Outside there was a gusty wind blowing and the bare trees made eerie sounds like at the beginning of a horror movie. Sawdust swirled in mini tornadoes across the grey pavement, crashing into stacks of lumber. Sheet metal banged against the roof. A figure lurched forward from behind a shed, pulling up his fly.

It was the yardman, my least favourite one, a belligerent kid with tattooed knuckles and a diamond stud twinkling in his nose. He reached for my order paper, snatching it from my hand.

"How about you load the 2X6 pile and I'll carry the 2X4s over to the truck, OK?" I said.

No answer. I parked beside the 2X6 pile. The kid started hurling eight-foot lengths of 2X6 lumber into my truck with a vengeance.

"If one of those goes through my back window, you're going to be out about four hundred bucks!" I called to him.

"I know what I'm doing!"

I crossed over to him and said, "OK, stop. I will load these myself. Go get the 2X4s and leave them beside the truck."

The kid pushed me out of his way and I fell down. And because I had not put on a Band-Aid, when I hit the woodpile my thumbnail tore completely off. I felt the pain that I imagined I should feel as I looked in horror at my gory

Open Up The Wall

thumb. I looked up and it seemed to me that the kid smirking. If he was going to apologize, I didn't give him a chance, I was so intent on hurting him back. I stood up, pulled him around by his coat, took aim and punched the surly punk right on the stud in his nose. He fell backwards against the side of the truck.

And then, before my eyes, he turned into a young man that I had deliberately hurt. My anger disappeared, leaving me feeling ashamed of myself. I had just punched one of the workforce's insignificant. Anybody with that level of anger deserves some compassion, not a punch in the head.

I stood holding my bleeding thumb watching him.

He held both hands to his bleeding nose watching me.

Suddenly a gust of wind came up and a mini-tornado carrying two identical empty Doritos packages swirled between us and went skyward. We watched them dance past the streetlights and out of sight. And then we looked at each other again.

"You OK?" I asked.

"You're gonna fuckin' get it, you motherfucker!"

I was furious all over again. Grabbing his collar, I yanked him clear of my truck.

"Get the fuck away from my truck! I don't want you bleeding on my truck!"

I got in and drove back to the office, slipped past Ronnie's mom and went to the order desk and told Ronnie what had happened. When he saw my bloody thumb, both hands went to his crotch and he said, "Pukkapukka."

"What did you say?" I asked.

Ronnie put both hands back on the counter.

"Nothing ... it's too weird to go into ... but I feel other people's pain in my crotch."

Ronnie was mainly concerned about any damage to my truck. We went back to the yard and he helped me finish loading. He said nothing to the kid, who was pacing furiously close by.

"I'd better let him cool off some more," said Ronnie. "Crazier than a shithouse rat, that one. Really pissed about being laid off. "

Ronnie didn't have to concern himself with customer relations anymore, so he said "See ya" and then turned his back to me, unzipped his fly and peed into the storm drain. A feeling like I could throw up was coming on strong as I accelerated out of that unfortunate place.

So many of life's unlucky find their way into manual labour. 'Lucky' for them will be a steady job lifting and carrying. They will be lucky if they ever figure out why they are so angry all the time, because they will get laid off a lot, and they will get fired a lot. They will get used to being treated with disrespect.

When you know what to look for, you can see it — the defeat in their body language as they trudge, dirty and tired to the subway. So much rage in their furrowed brows as they stand smoking at bus stops.

And I just punched one.

No one knew about this incident for years. My behaviour was so upsetting to me that I kept it to myself. Well-brought-up white guys with good teeth and university degrees do not go around contributing to the existential angst of the unskilled labourer.

In the years that followed, whenever I hired casual labour, what Lord Elmer Lytton dared to call 'the great unwashed', I made a point of paying helpers, framers, and drywallers above

Open Up The Wall

minimum wage and I never raised my voice to them. At least there was some upside to acting like a rich white prick that day.

My thumb had grown another nail by the time Greg laid me off from the house in front of the ice house. Stan had given me a lot to do and under his guidance I had patched the walls, installed the doors, assembled the IKEA kitchen, wrestled all the made-in-China light fixtures into place, and installed the baseboards and door trim. I paid close attention to the electricians and plumbers and absorbed all that I could. Whenever possible, I eavesdropped on the client/contractor conversations and I learned the absolute necessity for constant communication.

There is an order and flow to doing a full house renovation and I had traveled through it from start to finish, at times being trusted to take initiative and get things done on my own. I had learned from the best and I was grateful for the feeling of accomplishment that came with this new life full of daily surprises and challenges.

Except that two weeks later, I was out of work.

A full thirty-four days went by before I got another call.

At some point in my hiatus, it occurred to me that I could be doing some of this stuff on my own.

"I need to drum up some business," I said to Dixie. "I need clients of my own."

"Ah ... so you want to move from having a job to having a career?"

"Yeah, are you cool with that?"

"Yeah ... but no ponytail, no tattoos, and watch your language in front of the kids."

It ended up being a moot discussion. I couldn't find any work. Thank God Greg called.

Ten: The Real Deal

"I've got an addition up the freeway," Greg said. "You in?"

"Absolutely."

"Stan will be there, but you'll be working with Ken. Ken is a master carpenter and he's an absolute genius, so you are going to learn a lot. The thing is ... he takes some getting used to. Whatever you do, don't piss him off, because he can be dangerous."

Stan picked me up in his beat-up van, affectionately called "Old Blue," and we drove to the subway to pick up Ken.

On the corner, smoking furiously, was a man in a tank top, cutoffs and work boots. He stood about 5'4" with a slight, but muscular build, and a mullet.

"That's him," said Stan. "You'd better get in the back."

I clambered into the back and sat on the floor with the tools while Ken got in the passenger seat. He gave me a scowl, but said nothing. There was a sweaty/boozy smell to him.

"Good to see you, Ken," said Stan. "How you been?"

"Been in rehab."

I waited for a chance to introduce myself, but Ken rolled out the drawings and began to complain about the roof design.

From my vantage point on the floor in the back, I could see that Ken's shoulders bore the scars of bad

Open Up The Wall

adolescent acne. He held the drawings like he was reading a newspaper and I saw that his left forearm was covered with small scars from wrist to elbow. Further up his arm was tattooed the word MAYHEM. On his belt was a large folding knife in a leather pouch. Once he looked back at me, but didn't speak. He sighed constantly and on the exhale would say:

"It's all gooood."

We pulled up to a real live construction site. Beside a mid-sized bungalow was a vast new concrete block foundation. Surrounding it were ladders, scaffolding, stacks of lumber, a cement mixer ... I couldn't believe that I was actually going to build a house from the ground up. Look at me, Ma! I'm one of those common tradesmen you warned me about.

We all gathered around the drawings. Page one made sense, it was easy to see the addition beside the existing house. Page two showed how the new roof attached to the old roof. But when Stan and Ken started discussing the slope and the pitch, pointing to strange symbols, I was lost. I kept my mouth shut and nodded my way through pages three to seven.

Finally Stan said, "Let's get to it."

"OK! What do you want me to do?" I asked.

"I dunno. What CAN you do?" snorted Ken. "I mean, you look all clean cut, and you can't read drawings, and your hands are really smooth. What are you here for?"

"I've done a lot of interior framing, so I won't slow you down, if that's what you're worried about," I said firmly.

"This is house framing! You don't even have a framing hammer!"

"Aah, Ken ..." said Stan. "Geoff was abandoned at

birth, so you have to give him a break. Be nice, OK?"
Ken's eyes darted between us.
"What?!" he shouted. "What the fuck?! What the fuck are you talking about?"
Ken closed his eyes, inhaled slowly through his nose, exhaled, and sighed, "It's all goood."
Then he suddenly opened his eyes and said, "Fuck it! I don't want to know. Let's do this."

We began by building the walls for the first floor, working from the outside walls in, to the partition walls for all the rooms. The walls got assembled on the floor with studs spaced every 16", except where there was a door or a window. Then the wall got covered in plywood and lifted into position. This was done by resting the top of the wall onto the steel toe of our boots, which was just high enough off the ground to get a good grip. Then, on the count of three, it was lifted into place right at the edge of the floor, smacked into position by framing hammers on either side. Then the claw end of the framing hammer was swung into one of the studs at about head height, to get a grip on the wall and keep it from toppling over the edge, until it could be secured and braced.

Ken told me the story of the time the wind got a wall and it was teetering on its way to the parking lot below when he saved the day by whacking the claw of his hammer into the centre stud and pulling the wall upright again.

"If I'd had your hammer it would have been a fucking disaster. You can't get *lacksydaysial* when it comes to the right tool for the job."

On my way home that night I went to Home Depot to buy a framing hammer. They are longer and heavier than the

Open Up The Wall

normal hammer, designed so that its weight does the work, not your arm. They have long, almost straight claws for biting into wood. The head is fatter than a standard hammer, with a waffle texture for nailing accuracy.

"Who thinks this stuff up?" I asked myself as I pondered the evolution of the hammer.

"This is the latest thing," said the guy in the Home Depot apron — Tony, with the unfortunate title of "Tool Associate."

He showed me a lethal-looking hammer with a slight curve on the bottom part of the handle.

"You can swing this bitch all day and not get tired, because of this ergonomically designed handle."

"It feels good," I said. "You sold me."

Tony looked around before he spoke, as if he had a secret to share.

"Here's the thing. You have to get used to the different centre of gravity with this hammer, so take some time and give it a few practice swings before you get down to business."

Ken said the curve made my new hammer look gay. Then he quickly corrected himself. "I can't say that no more because my kids say it's bad and I am NOT *treadjeidist* but this is the kind of legal shit that my wife can use against me to get back custody of the kids, the lazy witch!" (Big breath.) "It's all gooood." And again, "It's all gooood."

He sniffed hard and wiped his eyes.

He said, "Lemme see." So I handed him my hammer, warning him about its balance and how the tool associate had said to practise a few swings.

"For God's sake," said Stan. "It's not a golf club."

We had left a couple of walls lying on the deck overnight. Now we began to lift the first one into position. I pulled out my new hammer from my tool belt and, aiming the claw side at a spot above my head, I swung the hammer back, right into the middle of my forehead, knocking myself onto to the deck.

Ken doubled over with laughter. "The wall!" Stan cried. I jumped back up and sank the claws into a stud. Ken did the same and we pulled the wall back from the brink. But Ken was laughing so hard that the wall started coming back on top of us. Stan shouted, "Put it back down!" We lowered it back onto the deck.

"Oh fuck! That's the funniest fucking thing I've ever fuckin' seen!" screamed Ken. "I wish I could fucking see it again in fuckin' slow motion fuck that was so fucking funny you have no fucking idea, oh my fucking Jesus how fucking funny was that oh fuck."

Finally, a happy reaction from Ken. It made me laugh with him. That such a Geoffrey move could take him out of his resident anger for even a moment was worth the pain in my head.

Ken kept laughing long past the appropriate amount of time. Then he said:

"And you want to leave me alone with this guy?"

A chill went through me and I turned to Stan. "What's he saying, Stan?" I asked.

"Greg wants me back at the ice house for a few days, so Ken can ride with you, and you guys can get the interior walls up and then do the rafters."

"And you look after all the delivery paperwork," said Ken. "I'm not too good in the reading department." He laughed an embarrassed apologetic laugh, then swung

Open Up The Wall

onto a ladder and got back to work.

I looked hard at Stan.

"Sorry," he said. "I just found out. Just don't piss him off and you'll be fine."

Ken was pissed off with me anyway, just for being born luckier than he was. He tolerated me, because it was clear to him that I was in awe of his skill. Over the next few days, I learned an astonishing amount from Ken. I watched his efficiency with his tools and his economy of movement on the deck. He had to explain a few things to me, because not only was I doing things that I had never done before, but there were also products that I had never seen before, like roof trusses and engineered timber. Ken's instruction always started like this:

"Not like that, you fucking ..."

But before his castigation was completed, he would stop himself, take a deep breath and sigh, "It's all goood." Then he would show me the right way to do whatever I had been doing wrong. But the sighing mantra thing was starting to irritate me so I told him that if he felt more comfortable yelling at me than sighing at me, I was fine with that. Then I imitated his "It's all goood."

That was a big mistake. Ken went ballistic, shouting at me inches from my face:

"I'm supposed to never stop doing that!! This is anger management, you fuck! You fucking motherfucking fuck! It's part of fucking rehab! I have to notice every time I'm angry and focus on the GOOD. Get it, fuck?"

"I had no idea. I apologize. What do you mean – the good?"

"I don't know ... Just ... like normal good, I guess ... That sort of bullshit."

"Can you be more specific?"
"What do you mean, *pacific*?"
"Never mind."

The heat was intense that summer. We were doing eight-bottle days. That means that we could drink eight bottles of water before we had to pee. I knew nothing about heat stroke, its signs or symptoms, but it was clear to me that if anybody was vulnerable to its effects, we were. I was concerned, because we were putting the roof rafters on now, and it seemed pretty dangerous walking along a 6" board, three storeys up, with no shade. I didn't know if this was a normal working condition for framers, but Ken wasn't complaining, so I just got on with it.

By mid-morning I was getting weary lifting the 12' long timbers into place. By lunchtime I was having trouble getting the 8' timbers into place. We came down the ladders and into blessed shade. I glugged a bottle of water and told Ken that I wouldn't last working through the heat of the day until 5:00.

"Then you'll get fired."

"I think that this is a safety issue now. We are both getting weak."

"We haven't finished the roof! We'll get fired!"

"Ken! You will not get fired for taking this kind of heat seriously. Besides, it's a bigger hassle for Greg if you get killed on the job."

Ken was frantic. He pleaded with me:

"We have to finish! I need this job! We'll take it nice and slow! OK?"

Even though I knew that his fear of getting fired was utterly irrational, his crazed certainty got me

Open Up The Wall

worrying that he knew something that I didn't. With mixed feelings, I relented. I was reluctant to make the call to Greg and say that we were too hot to work because I didn't know the procedure for this type of situation. But it seemed to me that only an idiot would work two storeys up on a narrow 6" walkway in the middle of a heat wave.

We doused ourselves in water and climbed back on the roof. Our progress was in slow motion. After an hour and ten minutes, I pulled out my tape measure, just as I had been doing all day, only this time I couldn't remember what I was doing. Was I measuring for a wall? A window? A roof? I couldn't remember!

That was it. I called to Ken to get off the roof. I was expecting an argument, but he carefully walked to the ladder and started down, fretting all the way.

"We are so fucking fired! Jesus Christ! What am I gonna do now? Greg is gonna be so mad when he hears we quit early! Oh fuck what am I gonna do? We are so fucking fired I mean .... aww fuck!"

My heart went out to him ... until he shook his mullet, spraying me with his sweat.

"Ken! Calm down! Greg will not fire you! You are a valuable asset to him and I know that he doesn't want you to risk your life up there. Now listen, it was my call to quit early so you can say that you had to quit too because I am your only ride back to town. OK?"

"Oh God I don't know! It's all so fucked now! Fucking heat! Fucking sun! Why me? Fuck!"

Then: "It's all gooood."

The route home down the freeway went past a series of subdivisions under construction. I pointed out to Ken that there was not one framer to be seen on any of the roofs of the half-finished homes.

"See? It's even too hot for those guys. They all got called down off the roof."

Ken leaned forward, rocking.

"Thank God. Thank God."

After a bit, he sat upright, leaving a sweaty imprint of his forehead on my dashboard. "What about you?" he said. "You could still get fired. It was your decision, right? I mean you made the call. I had to come with you because you're my ride home. What else could I do? Right?"

Ken's hand-to-mouth existence made this crazy fear of getting fired understandable. House framing doesn't pay well at all. It is usually volume work, like subdivisions. The worst part about the job is the pressure to work fast because, at the end of the week, the slowest guy will get fired. This would account for Ken's anger towards me when I did novice things that slowed down his productivity. It would explain how he could have no understanding of his value as a skilled tradesman. He was infected with a low-grade fear that at any time he could be out of work and, very soon after that, out of food.

We drove in silence past little cul de sacs with luxury homes under construction. The irony of the situation did not escape me. All these homes were being built by people who would never own a house in their lives. All of the craftsmen who built these buildings from the ground up, all the Kens in all the trades — from framers to masons, to tilers to cabinet makers — all with their unique skills, would never be acknowledged as anything more than those worker types that we don't

Open Up The Wall

think much of.

I drove Ken to the subway to go back to God knows where.

"Nothin' like a fuckin' Friday, eh? Feel so fuckin' free, eh?"

"Sure do. ... It's all goood."

"Haha very funny. Thanks for the ride."

"You're welcome. See you Monday."

"Yeah ... and don't you get too drunk this weekend, because you are going to have to haul some serious ass next week. You got a lot of time to make up for because you quit early today, you pussy!"

I was grateful for two days away from Ken. In spite of all that he was teaching me, his anger and his shame made him say such stupid, irrational things that by the end of the week I was worn out trying to make sense of him.

My thoughts turned to a hot shower and a cold beer. Together. Stan had turned me on to taking a beer into the shower. All my life I had showered in the morning when I woke up. The stumbling, dozey duty was something to be hurried through before I could get some coffee. Now I looked forward to the satisfying ritual of standing in the shower after work and watching my day dissolve into soapy grey water and stream off me. I sniffed the steamy air until the smell of sweat and sawdust was replaced by the scent of soap and shampoo. And then, to twist the cap off the cold beer and savour the new aroma, feeling the cold brew in my hand and the hot shower on my aching shoulder, was to enter a brief state of bliss. Just me, drinking beer, alone, with only the sound of water. It was a brief, beautiful time for mind and body to come together again.

By now, the excitement of being on a REAL construction site was gone. Framing was hard work. But worse, it was repetitive work. And worse than that, it was the kind of repetitive work where I couldn't afford to let my mind wander. Exact measurement and precise cutting in the intense heat required considerable focus. I had made a point of studying the drawings on my lunch breaks and by the time we got to framing the second floor I was up to speed. Not Ken speed, but I kept my end up. I had accepted that Ken did not look on me as his co-worker but as his bitch. I was happy with this relationship as long as I kept learning about framing, and I took his oblique insults:

"You should be working indoors ... maybe painting or something like that ... because you're destinied to fuckin' kill yourself up here."

His questions to me were sometimes topics for discussion, and sometimes unanswerable.

"You got your high school, right? Do you think people who don't have it look up to you? Like do you think they think you're better than them?"

"How come you have a truck and I don't, but I'm a better carpenter than you?"

Two weeks later, I dropped Ken and his oppressive pain and anger at the subway for the last time.

We each said, "Bye." Nothing more. We never saw each other again.

Eleven: Finding Purpose

At its core, acting is a victim's profession. Despite all their training and all the preparation that they put into every audition, at the end of the day, all an actor can do is hope they get the job. Despite all the voice classes, movement classes, and scene study classes, they still know that their success depends upon the approval of people far removed from the creative process — casting agents, producers, and financial backers. As a working actor, I lived with the low-grade anxiety of knowing that I would not get a job until somebody first approved of my physical appearance. Because landing a part is such a crapshoot, the audition process became a degrading ritual.

As a builder, owning my own existence and working on my own terms brought a peace of mind that I could never have imagined. At this point in my journey, I was secure in the knowledge that I had a set of skills that was in demand. Learning the trade from talented honourable men had given me confidence in my abilities, and in myself, making me want to stay in this world and grow. But, I was raised a Geoffrey, so I had some residual qualms about forsaking my artistic background and throwing my life away by becoming a common tradesman.

Then my neighbour David called. His wife had

died two years earlier and for a time there, he truly was a lost soul.

"I have a girlfriend," he said.

"That's great news, David! I'm happy for you."

"Thanks. Now ... this is important. I need my bathroom done before she will sleep over. It's not fair that I'm always at her place, just because my bathroom is a mess."

"Are you asking me to clean your bathroom?"

"It's a bit late for a cleaning."

David was a well-groomed man. His house was a pigsty.

Two years of dealing with grief and loneliness had taken his focus away from anything but the basics of housecleaning. He was getting it together with the rest of the house, but it would take a sandblaster to clean his bathroom fixtures. We agreed that all of them had to be replaced, along with the floor and the cupboards and the lights, even the switches. And all in record time.

I felt as though I had a cause. I was not just framing an anonymous structure to be inhabited by people that I would never meet. I was helping a man reclaim his life. His happiness depended on how well I applied my skills to the task of redoing his bathroom.

This was the noble thought in my head as I tried to get a grip on the lip of his filthy bathtub. The soap scum buildup made it too slippery to grasp, so I scraped enough away to get a handhold and finally yanked the thing off the wall. I dragged it through the house and straight into my truck. The sink came next. Like most sink drains of the era, it was clogged with hair. As I carried it to the truck, black blobs of old hair dripped from the sink drain onto my pants. The smell was sixty years old.

Open Up The Wall

The base of the toilets looked a kind of pee colour and the floor beneath was rotten. There was some old macaroni on the back of the seat. It looked like macaroni. I hoped it was. I cut the floor bolts away and lifted the toilet onto a plastic tarp and dragged it to the truck, stench and all. Wrapping my arms around the toilet, I made the final lift into the truck. It slithered in my arms and slid onto the truck bed leaving a grey/green ooze on my sleeves.

I smelled funny and there were chunks sticking to the soap scum on my shirt. My pants looked like I had wet myself, and worse, there were thick strands of dried black hair sticking to my belt. In The Creature from the Black Lagoon they discreetly hide the creature's crotch bulge with dangling swamp foliage. That's what my front looked like now. I put a layer of garbage bags over the seat of my truck, and drove to the dump.

The city dump, or 'Transfer Station', is a noisy, foul-smelling, happy place. It is usually the last stop for all the renovators who have spent the day ripping out old kitchens, bathrooms, fences —you name it. It's a happy place because after the junk gets dumped, it's Beer O'clock!

I lined up for my turn on the scale. The truck was weighed, the fat lady passed me my yellow slip and I drove into the cavernous holding room for the city's garbage. I backed in alongside five or six other trucks and began to unload my junk. It was good and slimy and slid effortlessly out of my truck onto the concrete floor.

I tried in vain to wipe off my pants. The smell on my arms was overpowering. So I made a decision. Taking the box cutter from my tool bag, I sliced my pant legs open until they were wide enough to get off over my work boots. I emptied the pockets and threw my pants as far as I could up the twenty-foot-high junk pile, and then I slid out of my shirt and let it fall. Wearing only my underpants and work boots, I jumped into the truck and drove back to the scales for my weigh-out.

It was such a hot day that I was confident that I looked like just another labourer with his shirt off. The heat had also influenced my choice of underwear that day and I felt uncomfortably vulnerable in my teal bikini briefs.

I pulled onto the scale and waited for my receipt. The fat lady reached her arm out the window, dangling the receipt. I tried to reach it, but there was a foot between our hands.

"Can you reach out a bit more?" I asked.

"No."

"I wouldn't ask you to except that I have a bad back," I lied.

"So do I."

There was nothing else I could do, so I stepped out of the truck. The fat lady's hangdog expression suddenly turned to one of alarm. She gasped, threw my receipt at me, and slammed her window shut. I picked up my receipt and got back into the truck. There was such a prudish, disapproving expression on her face that I laughed out loud, which must have made me look really crazy.

"I can explain this," I called.

She shook her head frantically, mouthing "No!" Then she motioned me to move on. I took in the wonderful moment of knowing how batshit crazy I must have appeared to the poor

Open Up The Wall

woman and then, fearing that I might be breaking some decency law, I drove directly home.

It was a fulfilling, rewarding experience working on David's bathroom. We came up with a whole new layout and I built storage closets, added more lighting, and a tile floor, finally transforming the scummy place into something elegant and inviting. When it was done and he said "Great job! I love it! Thank you so much!" I felt a new and different sense of accomplishment. It was an exhilarating change from the iffy, suspicious feelings that come with receiving backstage praise — "I enjoyed your performance ..."

David's praise was direct and undeniable. We both knew the impact that a new bathroom was going to have on the rest of his life. I could see the good things that I had done. I could touch them.

Twelve: Legitimate Business

Stan had a reputation for good work and plain dealing. He undertook one job at a time and finished it before moving on to the next. But now, if somebody wanted a small job done and Stan felt that I could do it to his standard, he would recommend me. I was the one to meet the client and give a price, but it was understood that I was riding on Stan's coattails.

It didn't take long for the word to get out that I was doing "reno stuff" and that I had the endorsement of STAN and, slowly but surely, I began to establish a client base of my own.

There was still doubt remaining in the minds of many prospective clients, especially the ones who only knew me as an actor.

"Stan said to call you about putting in a new door. Can you really do that?"

"Yes."

"But ... really do it?"

"How do you mean, really?"

"I don't know ... like a professional."

"I am a professional."

"Well ... um .... will Stan be around to oversee or anything?"

"No."

"OK then ... I'll get back to you."

I couldn't blame them, I guess. They had no idea of the hours that I had put in to reach a point where Stan would endorse me.

Open Up The Wall

My broker has CFP after his name. My masseur had RMT. The Wizard of Oz gave the Tin Man a heart. I needed a symbol that would inspire confidence. I needed a licence.

So off I went to city hall and filled out a stack of application forms, got a police background check and wrote an exam as to my abilities, followed by an oral exam, complete with trick questions. $325 later I had a licence with my picture on it. Then I got business cards with the words LICENCED CONTRACTOR prominently displayed. This seemed to reassure people that I was taking my career change seriously.

However, in spite of my new symbol of legitimacy, there was still the general anxiety that homeowners had about being overcharged for shoddy work by a contractor who seemed nice, took a deposit, half-finished the job, and then evaporated into thin air – just like they had seen on TV.

In a few short years, reality shows have turned the contractor into a pariah and put the homeowner on the defensive. This is characterized by what we called "The Look." It is the wary, almost disapproving look on the faces of prospective clients as they let me into their homes for the first time.

Fear of being ripped off is a two-way street. I can glean very few clues about how honourable or emotionally stable a new client is when I walk into their homes for the first time. There are stories about tradesmen being threatened with false allegations of sexual misconduct unless they give a better price, or having the odd tool stolen by a client. Every single one of us has at least one story about being cheated by people who "seemed very nice."

For me, the most enjoyable part of this business is working with homeowners, fleshing out their projects and getting to know them as people. Still, they have to be regularly reassured that I am trustworthy and competent. And I, in turn, have to be regularly assured that they completely understand every single step in the process of their renovation. At times I have made assumptions or been too casual in my communication, only to watch 'The Look' return to my client's face. Then everything stops while we all sit down and I explain myself more clearly, or physically show them that they are not being ripped off.

When I feel 'The Look' on my own face, it is usually because something doesn't add up to normal. I felt it when I went to Elsa and Tim's beachfront home. This was our first meeting and I was unnerved to see small cameras on tripods strategically placed throughout the spacious bungalow.

"Are you in the film business?" I asked.

Elsa laughed. "The cameras? They're for the dog," she said. "For a couple of weeks now, we've been coming home to all the cushions pulled off the couch, all the blankets off the bed — stuff he never did before. So the breeder put these cameras around to look for activities that can tell us if Milo is in pain, or anxious or frightened by something. It's for two to three days. And yes, I know that I sound like a crazy lady."

Milo, the huge Irish wolfhound, ambled into the room. He ducked his massive head into my 32 inch inseam, almost lifting me off the ground.

"Hello," I said. "What a beautiful dog you are."

"You're hired!" laughed Elsa.

Open Up The Wall

I sat on the couch across from Elsa and Tim and they told me that they wanted the carpet replaced with hardwood flooring. Milo stood staring at me, almost at eye level, while we talked details and timing and I gave them a square-foot price. I couldn't get any clues about them, as both of them were wearing running gear. They hadn't volunteered what they did for a living when I asked if they were in the film business, and I couldn't tell if they were avoiding telling me, so just to be on the safe side, I asked for a one-third payment up front.

While Tim wrote a cheque, Milo put his head on my lap and I rubbed his ears. When I got up to leave, he resisted and tried to heave himself onto my lap.

Elsa said, "Just whack him off."

I didn't respond.

Milo took an active interest in my work, staying close by my side while I tore out the carpet, swept up and put my big compound mitre saw in the middle of the floor. He was a warm-hearted dog and I liked having him around. I ate lunch sitting on the floor, with Milo lying right beside me. When I moved to get up, he rolled over and lay across my knees.

"Get off, Milo!" I said, and pushed at his big head a few times, but he just lay there panting at me. I was forced to wriggle myself free from under the beast's body. The dog sat up and licked his balls.

I got back to work and Milo followed me around for a while, then he began to pace and pull at the rolls of torn-up carpet, violently shaking the pieces. At one point, I looked up to see him on the couch pushing cushions to the floor with his hind legs. A short time later I was on my knees in front of my saw when Milo came up behind me.

He began pawing at my back, panting. I reached my left arm behind me to push him away, and that was the moment that the big dog decided to mount me, pushing forward against my saw and pinning my right arm against it.

"Get off me," I groaned. "Off ... off ... OFF! "

But Milo began humping me in earnest, panting his dog breath into my ear. For the life of me, I could not think of a way to get this dog off me, given my weak and precarious position bent over a saw. I continued trying to free myself from his attentions, but really, I knew that there was nothing I could do but let Milo have his way with me.

As far as I was concerned, this was a mildly amusing incident of no consequence ... until I remembered the camera to my left.

YouTube. America's Funniest Home Videos. Facebook.

Yes I would look ridiculous, but had I done anything that could be incriminating? Was I rough with the dog? Could the SPCA get me for anything? No. I was pretty sure that I was clear on all counts.

Milo finally dismounted and paced the perimeter of the living room for a while, before moving on to the king-size bed, where he paced in circles until he tangled the sheets into a ball. I shut him in the bedroom and continued laying the floor.

"Is Milo neutered?" I asked Elsa and Tim when they came home.

"No. The breeder wants to use him once before that happens. Why?"

I took a breath and said, "I have something to show you."

Tim hooked the living room camera to the TV and

Open Up The Wall 99

rewound until I said "There." The two of them sat on the couch together and Tim pressed PLAY.

There I was on all fours, bent over my saw, with Milo bent over me. The black and white footage looked like a vintage porn video, capturing a bizarre threesome of man, dog, and machine. In unison, Tim and Elsa said, "Oh my God!" before they burst into loud laughter.

The whole thing was over in twelve seconds. Time enough for Elsa to end up on the floor, doubled over laughing.

"I'm going to pee my pants!" she cried, and shuffled off to the bathroom.

Tim said: "When you were trying to push Milo and shouting 'Off - Off – Off ' it looked like you were really getting into it!" His laughter was in short gasps, and he called to Elsa in the bathroom, "Didn't Geoff look like he was getting off on it?"

Elsa howled from the bathroom. When she came out, she said "Oh by the way, nice floor" – which sent the two of them into further gales of laughter.

"Stick around while I call the breeder," said Tim. "We have to sort this out right now. We can't have you getting buggered again tomorrow, can we?"

The joke was wearing thin, but I laughed politely.

"I'm serious," Tim said. "You could have been hurt today."

Elsa gave me a glass of wine while Tim arranged that Milo would return to the breeder for a few days, and I would resume work when the dog was gone.

When I returned, there was a bottle of wine with a bow on it and a note which read: "Many thanks for a gorgeous floor, and for being such a good sport! All recordings are deleted." I was so touched by their care and consideration, that with the scraps of leftover flooring I built them a pagoda birdhouse for their Japanese garden.

    Almost one year to the day later, I was back to remove the tub from the guest bathroom and put in a shower for Milo, complete with two hand-held sprayers. The poor dog had been neutered since our tryst. He lay close to me as I worked and licked me when I patted him, but he never once circled me or looked at me with a glint in his eye.

Thirteen: Hey, It's Christmas

I was spending a lot of money on tools. When I put an outside plug on Sheila's deck, I had to buy a hammer drill to bore through the double brick wall of her house. That cost me $120. Then there was the $25 drill bit required for boring through masonry. I could only charge $90 for the job.

I used my new drill the next week, boring a 4" hole for a dryer vent. This time I had to buy a 4" hole saw for $45.

This was on a Friday. I was in a second-floor bathroom in a residential neighbourhood. I drilled the hole with my cool new hole saw and hooked up the new dryer. Then I set to replacing some cracked tile around the toilet. It was around 2:00 p.m. when the homeowner's daughter came home from high school with about six friends. It is the norm for latchkey kids to skip school on Friday afternoon. If I knew that a client had teenagers in high school, I expected it.

The girls all settled in the kitchen and I heard them calling out a watermelon vodka martini recipe. There was laughter and excitement at their illicit freedom, and it was music to my ears. I felt a wistful smile on my face as I tiled my way towards the bathroom door.

I heard footsteps in the hall behind me, then the exclamation "Oh!" from a girl in Grade 11. It is pronounced "Aeo."

I was on my hands and knees, so I stood up to address the young lady.

"Hi. I've taken the toilet out for a while, but there's one in the basement. I'm sorry."

She said "Aeo ... um ... thank yew" and went back down the stairs.

As she crossed to the kitchen, I suppose she thought that she was out of earshot. But I heard "EEEWWW!!! EEEWWW!!!"

The gaggle of girls reacted to her cry of alarm.

"What's happening?" "Omigod!" "Are you alright?"

She said: "EEEWWW! There's this OLD WORKER GUY upstairs in the bathroom!!!"

"EEEWWW!!!" X 6.

"Seriously! I didn't know he was there??? I just came up the stairs, and there was this, like, old man's ass in my face???"

"EEEWWW!!!" X 6.

"I'm serious! He's like, kneeling on the floor with his ass in the air!!!"

"EEEWWW!!!" X 6.

The young ladies stayed in the kitchen mixing drinks and talking quietly, but in the end OLD WORKER GUY drove them all out of the house.

Now that I spent my days in dirty, stained clothing, often with some kind of debris in my hair or dirt on my face, I began to realize that I was what the general population chooses to avoid, like vomit on a sidewalk - we see it, but instantly our energy goes into not seeing it. The Girl Guides outside the grocery store never approached me to buy cookies anymore. The veterans didn't offer to pin a poppy on my greasy jean jacket.

Open Up The Wall 103

Special interest groups outside the liquor store didn't want 'a moment of my time'. They let me walk right on by.

Old Worker Guys come across as too dirty to have money, or a social conscience.

Except at Christmas.

When people call in the days leading up to Christmas, it is always an emergency. Something is going wrong in their home and they see the situation as having the potential to ruin the holidays:

"My daughter was decorating the chandelier in the foyer and she accidently pulled it down!! We're having a reception on Thursday!! Of all the times for this to happen!!"

"The sprayer on my kitchen tap is leaking and I'm having twelve for dinner and the caterers say they won't come until I get a new tap!! Why does this have to happen now?"

These are the jobs that are a pain in the neck to do in April or October, because there is no money in driving across town to change a tap or hang a new chandelier. But at Christmas time, the Good Will Towards Men factor is in the air and I have trouble saying no, especially when they start crying.

I was replacing the cracked mirror behind the bar for a for a well-dressed woman who actually introduced herself as "the lady of the house" when a decorating service arrived with a completely decorated Christmas tree and a holly centrepiece for the vast dining room table.

When I was finished, I said, "That's a gorgeous tree."

"Goddamn thing cost a fortune," the lady of the house replied, before quickly apologizing. "I'm sorry, it's just that I'm up to my neck in all this Christmas crap. It is such a pain in the ass!"

This was something that I heard not infrequently. It seems that there is a portion of the population that feels put upon at Christmas time, as if they are making things nice for everybody but themselves. When things get tense, anything can happen. One December 21st I got this call:

"Yeah, is this Geoff?"

"Yes."

"Yeah, OK, I got your number from Janelle."

"Oh yes, Janelle, how is she?"

"Listen. I need a sink and toilet under my stairs — like a powder room off the kitchen. I need it for Christmas. So can you come around and do that? I'm going to be home tomorrow."

"I'm too busy to get it done before Christmas. I'm sorry."

"What do you MEAN you're busy?! OK FINE!!! FUCK YOU!!!" Click.

I was building a shelf unit for a longstanding client at his condo when Mohan, the security guard, appeared at the door.

"Got a minute?" he asked. "Mrs. Holt has a problem. It's her dishwasher. She lives across the hall. She wants to know if you'll take a look."

I crossed the hall into a condo filled with an extraordinary collection of antique pine furniture, making me stray further and further into this stranger's home, admiring the pieces. As I ran my fingers across a

Open Up The Wall

pine blanket box, a middle-aged woman wearing tight jeans, a crisp blue blouse, and extremely high heels clicked in from the kitchen.

"Oh, excellent!" she said. "Thank you so much for coming! Follow me."

The dishwasher door was open, revealing a gooey brown mass on the bottom and what looked like a fish head eyeballing me.

Staring into the dishwasher and cracking her knuckles, Mrs. Holt said: "I'm going to give you the short version ... I was poaching a salmon in the dishwasher ..."

My voice broke when I said, "Sorry ... What?"

"OK, go ahead and laugh," said Mrs. Holt. "But just so you don't think I'm some dumb old broad, I was following a recipe from a gourmet magazine. Anyway, the tin foil came off, or tore off, or something, and now I've got a salmon clogging my dishwasher. I ran it through a few times to try and flush it out, but then it just stopped completely. A very patronizing repairman said that he would be here yesterday, but he never showed up, and we've got my husband's family coming in."

I was still getting my head around fish in a dishwasher when Mrs. Holt cracked her knuckles and said, "So I'm asking you — can you fix it?"

"I can't, Mrs. Holt. I don't know how."

"Could you maybe clean it out so it will go a couple more times? Just until after Christmas?"

"I have a basic understanding of the working parts of a dishwasher, and if it has stopped working and filled with water, it is probably clogged beyond repair."

"What am I gonna do?" Mrs. Holt mused calmly.

Suddenly she hit her forehead with her hands, and moaned "I'm in big trouble."

I still had plenty to do on my other job, but I was in the building anyway. And hey, it's Christmas.

"The only thing I could do for you," I said, "is to replace this dishwasher with a new one."

"DO IT!" she said. "Oh God! If you can do it by tomorrow night, my husband will be none the wiser!"

The next morning, I loaded a new dishwasher into the truck and took it up to her condo. Mrs. Holt opened the door and gasped.

"You did it!" she cried. "I could kiss you, but we haven't been introduced, so I won't. What's your name anyway?"

I laughed and told her.

"Come on in, Geoff! Get that thing in here! We can make out later!"

She made me laugh, and I was feeling good about helping her out of a jam.

"First I have to get your salmon-clogged dishwasher out of here," I said, "and then I'll pop in the new one."

"It's gone," she said. "Security guy with the turban banged on my door at eight o'clock last night and said he would take it away. My guess is that he wanted it for the scrap metal, right?"

"That's a lot of trouble to go through for the five bucks he would get at the scrap yard," I suggested. "It sounds more like a random act of kindness to me. I mean- it's Christmas."

"Are you kidding?" said Mrs. Holt. "That type doesn't observe Christmas. He's just taking advantage of me. He just did it so I would be extra generous in his

Open Up The Wall 107

Christmas bonus. We all have to chip in for his Christmas bonus, you know, whether we want to or not. He knows it, and he's working it. It's a cultural thing with those types. It comes from the bazaars in their country where everybody tries to cheat everybody else. Even though he's probably been here for generations. Know what I mean?" She looked at me, nodding for agreement.

Ambushed by such unkindness, I am always at a loss for words, so I stood there feeling ineffectual and strangely alone. Mrs. Holt watched while I hooked up the dishwasher and slid it into place.

"Crisis averted!" she cried, and tottered down the hall in her pointy heels to a rolltop desk in the den.

"Come," she said.

I stood before her, silent and disappointed in humanity, while she wrote me a cheque. Then I left, missing the opportunity to tell her how much her unkindness had upset me, and hating myself for not defending the big-hearted security guard.

A conversation that I had had with Stan in early December came into my mind. We had spent a chilly morning putting in a huge picture window across from a parking lot full of Christmas trees. The Ghosts of Christmas Past became the topic of the day. I told him of coming home for the holidays, where the Christmas spirit in our house was so painfully forced that I couldn't wait to get back to boarding school. Stan told me of a childhood Christmas when he watched in horror as his mother glugged Scotch straight from the bottle while basting the turkey, and a short time later she passed out at the dinner table.

I called him.

"Compliments of the season to you."

"Is it time for the office Christmas party?"

"You and me, pal."

We sat in a worker-friendly bar and talked about the uncomfortable behaviour exhibited by some people around the holiday season. We soon drifted into Christmas construction memories, like the November that we built the false wall in the back of a couple's closet, so they had a hiding place for their four kids' presents, or when I built Little Red Riding Hood's bed for a Christmas pageant. After a couple of drinks, we canvassed the bar to come up with the year that Christmas went from being 'Christmas' to being 'The Holidays'.

Then we talked about how Christmas had found a place in our hearts again, now that we had kids of our own. We talked of Christmas concerts, Santa, stockings and the hyper level of excitement of Christmas Eve at bedtime, and shared the good feeling of knowing that we were doing a better job than our parents ever did.

At the curb we shook hands and had a man hug, bending forward from the waist. We said 'Merry Christmas' to each other and got into our beat-up vehicles. For me, it was just in the nick of time, because as Stan drove away I sat in my truck and cried. Not a lot, but I wasn't expecting it to come out so suddenly like that. I didn't have a health plan anymore, so I couldn't afford to have a shrink explain to me what the fuck was going on with my emotions around Christmas time.

Fourteen: Happy New Year

Along with Christmas emergency calls, December also brings the relaxed "In the New Year" calls. A homeowner in the planning stages of a project will get the ball rolling in the winter with a call to his contractor. Ballpark figures get floated around and the call always ends with an agreement to touch base "in the New Year"... which could mean January or July.

This January, the bases were loaded with some interesting and unique jobs, and some cool people.

In a notoriously upscale condo, Mrs. Pearson wanted floor-to-ceiling bookcases for the library that she was creating from a walk-in closet. She also wanted to try her hand at using a power saw.

"They kind of scare me, and they kind of turn me on," said the mother of three.

With some thought to liability, I said a cautious yes. The saw that I would be using is commonly called a "chop saw" and, as the name implies, it lowers a blade onto a piece of wood and chops it to size. It can't slip or fall, so as long as fingers are out of the way, nothing can go wrong.

"There will be sawdust," I said. "You might want to change."

"I'm good," she insisted.

"Well, OK, but for safety's sake, tuck your pearls into your sweater, do up your cardigan and don't wear your high heels."

She knelt beside me on the floor and paid attention to my instructions on how to safely lower the blade to the pencil mark on the wood. Her husband, Horace — Hore for short (!) — stood to one side with his cell phone camera. We went over safe hand positions and then I said, "When you're ready, fire it up."

She pulled the trigger and the saw screamed to life — and so did Mrs. Pearson. She screamed loudly through the whole cut. When she released the trigger, she shouted:

"Holeee! That was absolutely amazing! I don't want to think about what that could do to my fingers!"

More cuts and more screams. Hore mentioned that by now someone must have heard her screaming and think that she was being murdered.

"I have to scream," she said. "This is a thrill, like a roller coaster. Who doesn't scream on a roller coaster?"

I really liked Mrs. Pearson. My dilemma came when I had to run a wire through their son's bedroom closet. Hidden behind the shoe tower was a bag of weed and a bong. What to do? Precedent dictated discretion: The time I found a thick envelope of money dangling from duct tape on the underside of a chair, I taped it back up. When I discovered a cat batting a vibrator around a dining room, I took it from her and put it beside one of the bedside tables, reasoning that this was the general vicinity of where the thing lived.

This time, however, there was something at stake. The kid was twelve. I decided to leave everything out on the floor where I knew that his mother would see it. I don't know what happened. Nobody ever said anything to me about it, even though I was back to do work for the Pearsons many times in the years that followed.

Open Up The Wall

Delphine and Mitch were dancers/performance artists with a warehouse that they wanted to turn into a performance space. After I insulated the walls, I had a great time covering them with old fence boards, paint can lids, corrugated plastic and anything else that the dancers brought in from the garbage to turn boring walls into art installations. The hours were erratic, because I couldn't work during the dance classes, but I didn't care because I was doing crazy things like building a low-level stage while a videographer filmed a couple dancing around me.

The last of my 'In The New Year' jobs for this year ended in the most bizarre of injuries.

Mrs. Mason wanted her spare bedroom turned into an office, and I had built her a long desk, deep enough to cover the radiators against the wall. I was on my knees under the desk, bolting it to the wall when I heard Mrs. Mason say something like "That looks nice." She was on her way from the shower, wearing a towel. The towel was too short, and Mrs. Mason stood too close to the table. I turned to face a freshly showered hairy bush!

I cried out a non-word, like "Gaa" or something, and then swung my head down and to the right, in order to avoid the full frontal visual. I felt a sudden searing pain in my neck and shooting down my left arm. But worse, there was the ringing of warning bells in my head. This could be the nightmare scenario that contractors talk about. Was Mrs. Mason doing this deliberately? Could this possibly be the subtle start to suggesting an alternative method of payment? What if it was all totally innocent, but Mrs. Mason realized that I must have seen up her towel and got mad and fired me, or told her husband the lawyer that I was a pervert? With absolutely no idea of what to do next, I drew my knees to my chest and waited under the desk for Mrs. Mason to make the next move. When she came into the room fully clothed a short time later, I crawled out from under the desk, relieved that nothing was going to change in our relationship, and that I would not be arrested for anything to do with an old worker guy alone with a naked woman. But my neck was killing me.

"You have a herniated disc in your neck," said Peter the physiotherapist. "Tell me what happened?"

I got as far as: "This woman wearing a towel came in …"

"Got it," said Peter. "The woman was your mother, your sister, your boss, someone like that. You saw her naked, and had an extreme reaction to her nudity. It's a common scenario."

"Are you serious?!?"

"Oh yeah. Somebody walks in on somebody naked in the bathroom, and they freak out, turn too fast and break their nose on the door jamb, or the other one slips in the shower trying to cover themselves. You need an X-ray."

The prognosis for a complete recovery was some time 'In The New Year'.

Fifteen: The Addition of Death

Stan called me in June about working with him on a second-storey addition. That is, taking the roof off a bungalow and building a second storey where the roof used to be, and then of course building a new roof on the new storey.

On the degree of difficulty scale, any addition above the first floor is a *10 out of 10*. For the general contractor, the stress level is way past ten. It is easier to build a new house from the ground up than it is to tear off a roof and tiptoe around on 2" wide joists, building another storey, with the family living below, separated by ½" of drywall ceiling. I had no idea what Stan was going through keeping this job moving, but as time went on I began to see a different side of my easy-going friend.

The first step was to get rid of the roof by cutting through the shingles and plywood with Skil saws, pushing them from the bottom of the roof to the peak, being careful not to cut the roof rafters. Stan had hired a third guy named Mason, and he carried the cut-up chunks of roof to the edge of the wall and pitched them into the dumpster below. Mason was a cellist and demolition was his day job. He always had his shirt off, so that the world could see the tattoo of a snake that coiled from the small of his back, under his arm and around to his belly button. Now, when I am at the symphony, I wonder about what is beneath a musician's formal attire. Why does that violinist always wear a long sleeved gown? Did I just see a flash of tattoo when the tympani player raised his arms?

Pushing my saw through the roof for the umpteenth time that morning, she suddenly stopped. Dead. I was very sad to see it die. It was my first power tool. We had started my new life together and I felt remorse at having taxed the poor thing too hard, so I took off the housing to see if I could fix it.

Stan called over from his side of the roof: "What's going on over there?"

"I burned out my saw. It's the first one I ever bought."

"Go get another one!" he said with some impatience.

I couldn't blame him. We were racing against the clock and the elements. A roof has to be completely removed in one day so that huge tarps can cover the floor, which is technically the ceiling of the floor below. Things are pretty tense for a couple of days until the new subfloor goes on where the roof used to be. At least at that point, there is a covering that won't blow away.

I roared off to the nearest big box store and bought the same kind of saw as Stan's — very precise, very heavy duty. $325. Then I roared back to the roof and worked through lunch because I could see that Stan was tense and I worried that it had something to do with me. I still regarded myself as a student of Stan's and I felt a constant need to please him.

When the roof was all sliced up and pitched into the dumpster, we had to walk on the 2" wide joists that spanned the width of the house and held the ceiling of the rooms below. We tiptoed across these joists while we screwed down a plywood subfloor on top. The joists

Open Up The Wall

were spaced 16" apart. Mason slipped and put his foot through the bathroom ceiling. Even though this is a somewhat regular occurrence when walking on roof joists, it was an expense that Stan would have to cover. He kept a sense of humour about it, I'm sure because of his accident a year earlier, when he fell through the ceiling of a bungalow into the kitchen below.

But then ...

It was as if God was out to test us, Old Testament style. First came the wasps, displaced from their nest in the rafters, swarming and stinging. With nowhere to escape, the best I could do was lie face down in the loose insulation between the joists, cover my face and get stung six times.

Then the gale force wind came up while we carried sheets of plywood across the roof. We fought to keep our footing as we walked on the 2" joists, praying not to lose balance and step through the ceiling again. But I did, and this time Stan was furious.

When we finally got the plywood subfloor glued and screwed, we were visited by torrential rains.

After a night of downpour, Stan called early.

"Get over here right now with every bucket, rag and mop you can spare."

We had covered the entire deck with thick plastic, and stapled it down before we left the day before. I don't know how, or where the rain got through, but it soaked the dwelling below. The hardwood floors in the hallway were warped beyond saving.

Stan was squeezing wet towels into a bucket. I took a bucket and started at the other end of the house. We did this in silence for a couple of hours.

When the rain stopped, we waited a day for things

to dry out and started framing the walls. Stan was having a lot of trouble cutting and fitting the dormers, and Mason and I frustrated him further by framing the window openings to the wrong dimensions. Each one of us had gashed our leg on the same nail sticking out from the stairwell, and we all considered this a bad omen. Nothing was going according to plan, and things were getting really tense.

While I was putting up short hip rafters on the roof, my long framing hammer prevented me from turning around in the tight space, and I was afraid that the damn thing was going to lever me right off the roof. To be on the safe side, I took the hammer from my tool belt and put it on the 5½" wide wall that I was standing on top of. Stan walked underneath — just as I turned my foot and knocked the hammer off the wall, narrowly missing his head. I was aware of how close I had come to killing him. So was he. We didn't wear hardhats. Nobody non-union wears hard hats. The thing is, I have never been in a situation, before or since, where I felt forced to take my hammer off my belt.

This job had bad karma all over it. I hated going to work. None of us liked each other anymore, and Mason and I were totally out of synch with each other's rhythms. I found myself longing for Ken.

The day after I considered the possibility that I could die on this job, Mason and I botched another wall. One small piece of plywood sheathing was missing from above the framed window and, incredibly, nobody had noticed. At this point I was starting to believe in evil spirits.

It fell to me to get a long, long ladder, go up and nail

Open Up The Wall

a piece of plywood into place above the second floor window frame. I had to put the ladder in the neighbours' yard to get a safe enough climbing angle, resting it on the window opening. Carefully pushing a 3'X2' sheet of plywood ahead of me, I climbed to the top of the window frame. That went well. I lifted the wood into position. That went well. I started nailing it into place. With the first blow of the hammer, I felt the ladder slip down.

I said: "Oh no."

The ladder said: " Oh yes! I'm slipping down. I guess you didn't notice that you put my feet by the neighbours' garbage cans. Greasy! Slippery!"

I froze.

"That's not going to help," said the ladder. "It's simple physics. I have to slide down to the ground. That means that you have to come up with a plan in about two seconds."

I watched as the top of the ladder slowly slid closer to the edge of the window. My only chance was to make a leap for the window frame, and pull myself through.

"Don't push off with your feet!" said the ladder. "That will send me flying. Frankly, I will be glad to hit the ground and have somebody put me away. I'm overextended as it is. I don't have to tell you, this job sucks! Everything is going wrong! Anyway, good luck, I'm outta here!"

I let myself fall forward and I just made it to the window frame as the ladder slid to the ground thirty feet below.

My chest and arms were over the window frame, but the rest of me dangled from the second-floor wall. There was no foothold for my feet, so I kind of inch-wormed my way up the window frame until my tool belt got caught on the windowsill. Somehow I got my knee on the ledge and rolled my body sideways through the window frame. When I finally fell to the floor, I was gasping for air and — I don't know why — I was furious.

Stan came and stood over me.

"What's going on? You hurt?"

I told him what had happened.

"Jesus! Why didn't you call me? I was around the corner, ten feet away!"

Nobody heard me because I didn't call for help. I didn't call for help because I had been holding my breath the whole time. What a weird thing to do!! Nothing was right about this place.

"This is all so fucked up!" I shouted. "Somebody is going to fucking die on this fucked up jobsite!"

Stan walked away.

When I went to get the ladder from the neighbour's yard, a man in a T-shirt with a picture of Ronald McDonald on it swung the door open.

He stepped outside and said, "This is private property!"

I dropped the ladder and let out a furious howl to the sky. Then I turned back to the neighbour, but he was already back inside.

The nights turned into sleepless hell as I was jolted awake by dreams of falling. Then I would lie awake going through what I had to do the next day and devising strategies as to how I could stay safe. I was waking up tired and going to work tense.

It didn't get any better. The owner of the house wanted to pitch in and help. Always a stupid move. He

Open Up The Wall

lasted a couple of hours before he had a serious accident, and spent the next three months with his arm in a sling. Stan was short tempered, and I was too inexperienced to understand the stress that he was under, dealing with the rain catastrophe and the insurance companies, all the while keeping the job moving forward. We were all polite with each other, but inside we wanted to kill each other. The devil was in our midst.

We were still framing and fixing stupid mistakes when Stan got a call. I heard him say, "You can have him right now." He got off his phone and told me to take all of my tools and go and do some carpentry for a man called Bruce.

That was the last I saw of Stan for two years.

Sixteen: No Turning Back

The voices in my head had a field day:

"Actually, you got fired. You didn't fit in. In the end, your mother was right ... Geoffrey. What you gonna do now? Go back to acting? You can't do anything else, can you? A commercial maybe? Perhaps you can be a spokesman for a cookie or something, because it has just been confirmed that YOU ARE NO GOOD WITH YOUR HANDS!!"

I had come so far that I knew I couldn't go back. I couldn't waste the excitement and the sense of satisfaction that this learning curve had given me. I had to take stock and figure out how I was going to proceed on my own.

On my own. It was a bit of a shock to think it out loud. Up until now, I had been an employee/student of Stan. Sure, I had gone off to do things on my own, but I always had the safety net of Stan's experience, and his friendship. I relied heavily on both.

"Hey, Stan, what's the code for stair-railing height?"
"Hey, Stan, could you show me how to do this?"
"Hey, Stan, can I borrow your planer?"
The safety net was definitely gone now.

I would have liked to have stayed home that night and prepare for my new job, but we had symphony tickets. The concert hall was crawling with Geoffreys, so I counted blazers for a while then I read the program notes on Anton Dvorak.

Open Up The Wall

Early in his career as a composer, he was supported and encouraged by Johannes Brahms, who wrote great symphonies but ended up famous for a lullaby. Only when Dvorak left the comfort of his mentor, and moved to America, did he focus completely on himself and write his *New World Symphony*.

That was what was going through my head! I wanted that to happen to me. I was desperate to stay in this business, to excel on my own, and find the kind of personal satisfaction that Anton Dvorak must have found when he finished his symphony and said to himself "Wow, this is really good. I never knew I had it in me."

Something like that ... anything like that! Because I wasn't going to quit working with my hands. I wasn't going to give up the sense of self-worth that this trade had given me. I was comfortable, at last, when I was building things and there was no way that I was going back to the life of anxiety and self-doubt:

"I hope they liked the audition ... I thought it went well ... They seemed to like me ... One of them smiled at me ... God I hope they give it to me."

I didn't want to wait for the phone to ring anymore. I didn't want to go to summer festivals and entertain rich people for six nights and two afternoons a week. I made my own schedule now. I had the ability to build people things that they wanted. I was articulate and considerate, and I had a fair number of tools. If I could just keep my insecurity at bay, I had the makings of a fulfilling life right in front of me.

The next morning when I went to meet Bruce, I was going as myself and not as Stan's helper. I followed a bent street sign that read 'Memory Lane'. A drug dealer and his pitbull watched me from the corner as I drove down what amounted to an alley filled with potholes and littered with empties. Halfway down, I found the address on the door of a cinder block warehouse, with a solid locked gate in front.

I pressed the buzzer and a voice came back.

"What?"

"I'm Geoff ... I ..."

"Oh! Hi! I'll be right out!"

A man came out of the door and walked towards the gate with a huge ring of keys in his hand. He was clean-shaven, with curly black hair almost to his shoulders. I recognized him. He was the drummer in a famous country rock band.

"Hey Geoff, I'm Bruce."

"I know!! Oh wow!! I still have you guys on vinyl!!"

"Cool. I own this place now. C'mon in."

Bruce let me in to a vast space, filled with amplifiers, cables, microphone stands, pedals and pre-amps. Whatever a band needed for a single gig, or a whole tour, Bruce could provide. He had also seen the need for a private space where a drummer could practise with his complete drum kit anytime, day or night, so my job was to build four small rooms, each one just big enough to house a full drum kit and a music stand. I was to wire for a plug and a light in each room and put on a door with a good lock. The drummers would be listening to the music tracks in headsets, so the little rooms didn't need to be soundproofed.

"How much?" he asked.

"Let me take some measurements," I said, "and then I'll get back to you."

An experienced contractor could have given a pretty

Open Up The Wall

accurate price, simply by basing it on similar type of jobs done in the past. Not me. I had no past on which to base anything. I would have to tally up the cost of every single board, screw and nail that was going into this job. It would be time consuming, but it's not rocket science. But if I were to leave something out, I would have to admit it to Bruce and then add the cost of my omission to his bottom line. Then 'Licensed Professional' would become 'Incompetent Old Worker Guy' in the blink of an eye. I lay on the wood floor of my living room and visualized every bit of material that I would need, then turned onto my stomach and wrote it all down. Now for the hard part — calculating how much to charge for labour.

"How many hours to frame the walls of such a structure? Well, I've framed a lot of walls, so I can probably get it all done in a day... so ... eight hours ... but I have to go and get all the lumber. Loading it all in here through the front door and down the hall is ... three more hours? Yes, 11 hours for framing. If I round it off to 12 hours, that will be 10 hours to do the framing, and two hours on the front and back ends for pickup, delivery and cleanup. That sounds high now. The doors are going to take time, because they all have to be cut down, so maybe I should push myself on the framing and leave the extra time for the doors. So ... OK, eight hours for framing. OK."

I fretted my way through every aspect of the job – lights, plugs, switches, insulation, drywall, doors, locks and trim.

"Oh God, I forgot to add in tax. That's going to bring the price up A LOT! Maybe I should just absorb the tax. No, no, no! If I go any lower, he will think that I am conning my way into the job by lowballing it now and then hitting him with extra costs later on, and then he won't trust me anymore. In the end, this business is all about trust."

I added and subtracted and thought and visualized for a couple of hours before I had a price that I was comfortable with. I emailed it to Bruce.

His reply came back immediately: "Start tomorrow 8:30 a.m?"

I was relieved and happy. I had escaped the Addition of Death, and I was going to do kind of work that I really enjoyed — turning an empty space into something useful, and really cool.

The next morning there was a beautiful summer sunrise as I pulled into a space in the 'Contractor Parking' section of the Home Depot. At 7:00 a.m., we builders have the place to ourselves for a couple of hours before the 'civilians' come in to buy their birdseed and picture wire. There is the smell of cigarettes, coffee, and lumber. There is laughter, and instructions being barked at helpers; there are lots of groans and sighs as lumber, or drywall, or bags of concrete get heaved into beat-up trucks and vans. This is how the trades start the day — loading material that will change a house. For the most part, it's an energetic, happy place because everybody who is there has a job.

By 7:45 a.m. I had loaded the lumber into my truck and was headed to Memory Lane.

Crackheads get up early too, so do dealers and their dogs, and by 8:15 Memory Lane was hopping. As I waited for Bruce to come and open the gate, a skinny woman offered to "do me" for ten bucks, and then a scary-looking guy checked out the tools in the back of my truck while he let his pit bull pee on the tire.

Bruce arrived and let me in. There was a forest of

Open Up The Wall

microphone stands where I was to build the drum rooms, so I moved a dozen or so out of the way and began bringing in the lumber just as Bruce began rolling huge speakers into the same space from the opposite direction. I moved all my lumber to a new spot.

"Don't touch a thing," he said. "It's all set to be loaded, and all this gear should be gone in half an hour or so."

With no room to work inside, I carried the wood outside again, lowered the tailgate on the truck and set up my compound mitre saw. It is the jewel in my crown of tools. A beautiful, precision machine that looks like a steel bird of prey, it has an upright, regal bearing, but tucked under its brow is a lethal band of teeth. Pull the trigger and it screams to life, diving down headfirst onto the exposed wood lying below. Just as quickly, it sighs into silence and springs back to its statuesque pose, ready to strike again. I care for this tool as a chef cares for his knives.

A young man came out through the loading door with some wood in his arms.

"Mind if I use your saw?"

"Yeah, I do."

"Okaaaay ... Bruce said I should cut these ... so ...like..."

"Let me cut them for you."

"Oh! Okaaaay ... I'm getting this now. Your saw is like my guitar — no touchee by noooobody! Am I right?"

"That's right."

"You and me, Bro!" He held out his fist for me to bump.

You and me, Bro. The brotherhood of gear. Each of us was defined by the tools of our trade. We stood facing each other for a few seconds. He looked at my toolbelt, while I counted the bracelets on his arm.

"Thanks for doing this, Bro," he said. "We're going to

rehearse in the Big Room, so I need these boards to make a ramp to roll in our gear."

The Big Room? That was where I was supposed to be building. I went to talk to Bruce.

"Yeah it's mayhem here today," he said, "so why don't you finish the windows instead."

"Windows? You didn't mention any windows."

"Well, yeah, I got new windows put in, but now they have to have all the trim put on the outside, and caulked before winter, so why don't you do that for now and get back to making the drum rooms whenever the Big Room is free. Cool?"

The windows were second-storey windows. Like at the Addition of Death. The 40' ladder clanged and rattled happily as I lifted it into position.

"How do you think you'll make out?" asked the ladder.

"Fine, just fine," I growled. "Once I get your feet firmly planted on the pavement."

The first thing to do was to take measurements, which meant that both hands would be off the ladder while I used the tape measure.

"Nothing can go wrong unless you panic," said the ladder. "Seriously, my function is to help you. I'm a tool, for God sakes. I'm built to help you, but I'm feeling such animosity here!"

"I don't trust you!" I said. "I never expected that you would try to kill me, so to me, you are definitely a big fucking tool."

"Oh be reasonable! You had one scare and you lived ... pussy."

I measured the first window and then I started back down. Except my feet wouldn't listen to my brain.

Open Up The Wall

"You have to move your feet, Geoffrey."

I really wanted to, but I couldn't decide how to start the process. I felt sweat on my hands, so I pressed myself against the ladder because I couldn't trust them to grip for me. Where was ME? All I knew was that I couldn't trust the guy on the ladder to move his feet down to the next rung.

The Curse of the Addition of Death had followed me here.

My estimate for Bruce's job was moot by the second day. I was moving from one added-on job to another and doing so many extra things that I just kept a list and spent the next few weeks working my way through it. One day I built little waist-high boxes to put amplifiers in, and the next day I built 8' high skinny cupboards to hold hundreds of cymbals. Every day was different, and not just the jobs. The whole tone of the building changed with each band that came in to rehearse. While I built touring boxes on wheels, and portable stages, I was privy to their rehearsals and felt their excitement build as new songs found a life of their own.

One morning I said my usual polite "Wazzup" to the dealer with the dogs and locked the gate behind me. As I got closer to the building, I could hear a scorching rockabilly tune coming from inside, and it thrilled me. I took the moment to appreciate how lucky I was to have a life that let me move in and out of so many other people's lives. A bit of a poem by Tennyson popped into my head. I hadn't thought of it since I had to recite it decades earlier at some library event.

"I am a part of all that I have met ..."

By mid-November I finished everything on Bruce's list. I

was sorry to leave the exuberant, creative environment of musicians and sound techies. Then again, the lounge acts were coming in to rehearse their Christmas shows. I packed up my tools and loaded out to a painfully mournful rendition of 'Little Drummer Boy'.

Seventeen: The Help

On to the next. By now I had jobs lined up in advance. My client list was growing and even though I knew that I would never have the fearless confidence of Stan, I was making forays out of my comfort zone and taking on more and more ambitious projects.

I still didn't have a crew to help me move things along. As a professional contractor I was incomplete, and it weighed on me.

An older couple, Mr. and Mrs. Vance, wanted to upgrade their thirty-year-old bathroom. New tile floor, new bathtub/shower, new window, cupboards. New everything.

There is only one way to redo a bathroom properly. The walls have to be opened up, right down to the studs, so that all the plumbing and wiring is exposed. Opening up the wall is the only way to see the ugly surprises behind it. And there is ALWAYS something. Apart from old galvanized pipe, or knob and tube wiring running behind the tub, I've seen a plug covered over with a tile, a garden hose used as a drainpipe, copper pipe held together with saran wrap and duct tape, and, of course, lots of mould. My waking nightmare is that if I don't expose these problems at the start they will come back to bite me later and I will have to rip out all my new work to fix them.

I gave Mr. and Mrs. Vance a price of $12,000 leaving myself a contingency of $2,000 for trouble behind the walls.

Mr. Vance had 'The Look'.

"How long will this job take?"

"Three weeks."

"That long?"

"Three weeks is pretty standard for a bathroom of this size."

"I had calculated six days."

I nearly choked. Was he trying to negotiate a time frame, or was he just naïve?

"I couldn't do it in six days," I said. "Perhaps that company that only does bathrooms might be a bit faster. You may have seen their ads ..."

Mr. Vance shook his head. "What's going to take so long?"

"I have a lot of structure to replace. Then it takes time to properly prepare and level the ninety-year-old floor and walls for the tile. If you want things to go faster, a linoleum floor can be ..."

Again he shook his head. "That would be hideous."

"Then it will take me about three weeks — fifteen working days."

"You don't work on the weekends?"

"No. I spend my weekends with my family."

"Well then, you'd better get started."

Mr. and Mrs. Vance could have stepped out of Grant Wood's painting American Gothic — the morose couple standing in front of their barn, the man holding a pitch fork. There was also the scent of Elizabeth Arden bath salts, awakening an eerie childhood memory.

The Vance home was immaculate. This told me that even the slightest departure from perfectly clean would be the wall between us. The first thing to do when working in someone's living space is to tape up sheets of plastic and put down drop cloths. This obviously contains debris

Open Up The Wall

and dust, but, more importantly, it reassures the client that they chose a professional who has respect for their home.

I doubled the drop cloths on the Vance floors and doubled the plastic on the walls until the place looked like an alien womb. After that, I began the process of loading in my tools.

In the back of my truck I keep my tool bag, a milk crate of power tools and a hockey bag of cordless tools. In my basement, I keep the table saw, the vacuum, the mitre saw, levels and six plastic tubs full of parts and material, each labeled in magic marker: PLUMBING – ELECTRICAL – DRYWALL – DEMOLITION – TILE.

For a bathroom job, every bit of this gear would eventually get loaded into Mr. and Mrs. Vance's second-floor hallway. On day one they have no way of knowing that by Day 15 they will be utterly fed up with me, my tools and the disruption in their lives. I know it all too well, so I know to keep a tight daily schedule. This means: Decline any offers of coffee or muffins. Do NOT stop for lunch. At the end of the day, pack all the tools into the bathtub space then vacuum and load the garbage out before they start making dinner.

I could feel myself putting pressure on myself. Under the circumstances, it was only natural, because periodically I would see Mr. and Mrs. Vance drift by. Together, they would peer through the plastic as I worked. They never spoke. Not even to each other. Just two silhouettes behind plastic ... standing there ... watching me ... never uttering a sound. It was all in my head that Mr. and Mrs. Vance would jump me and inject me with a sleep serum, roll me in my own plastic and watch me suffocate. My discomfort came from the fact that they gave away NOTHING. I couldn't tell if they were happy with what I was doing or not, and this kept me awake and made me worry. About what? That they didn't like me? Personally?

Well, yes, actually. It is really important that my clients don't DISLIKE me. I am the messy intruder into their lives, therefore a crucial part of my job is to make the homeowner comfortable with my presence. I have to be the one to build the trust between us so that they can't build a fear wall. Apart from expecting the job to be done on time and on budget, they are expecting me to disarm the alarm every morning when I arrive, pat the dog, and not let the cat out while I load in a ton of gear and material, sign for delivery packages, schedule quiet work for when the baby goes down, and give tours to curious neighbours. In other words, fit into their family lifestyle. It is an undeniably false relationship, like a never-ending second date, with equal parts of trust and wariness. But when the routine is established, and the walls come down, mutual respect is established and nice people come together.

As I opened up the plumbing wall and cut away the galvanized pipe, I regretted my decision not to call in a helper to haul out the debris and bring in the new material. It might have saved me a day overall, but Mrs. Vance had repeatedly brought up her concern about noise and dust, so I had decided to keep the lowest possible profile. Besides, I had John the plumber coming in to run new drains and put in the tub. That would be noisy enough.

John worked for a large plumbing company that had

vans with their logo on them and shirts with their names on them. We had identified each other as the only tradesmen in a lunchtime deli one day, so we sat together. John was a sculptor, working with metal for the last twenty-two years. Despite healthy sales, and the odd artist grant, he got his plumbing licence to support a wife and child. I viewed his impressive portfolio on his phone. He felt like a good fit for me, so I called his company and booked him for the Vance job.

On the day, they sent two other guys.

"Where's John?" I asked.

"Somewhere in the west end ... I don't know where," said the short one. "But we're all licensed plumbers, so it doesn't really matter."

"OK," I said. "Come upstairs and I'll show you the alcove I built for the drop-in tub."

They stood staring.

"Fuck," said one finally.

"Fuckin' tight, eh? Really fuckin' tight," said the other.

I could hear Mr. and Mrs. Vance on the floor below. I knew that they were unwilling auditors to this conversation.

"It is built exactly to the installation specs," I said, trying to keep the exasperation out of my voice.

The short plumber sighed dramatically, and said: "We'll get it in. I'm just saying it's pretty fuckin' tight."

"It is supposed to be tight," I said. "There can't be a gap, I'm putting tile around the tub. You must know that."

I knew that they were just complaining about having to work in a tight space, because the short plumber said,

"Well, yeah, but this is as tight as a nun's cunt! I mean, this is gonna be a fuckin' bitch for us!"

"Watch your mouth!" I hissed. "The homeowners are downstairs!"

"Oh fuck! Sorry!"

The tub fit perfectly, but the two of them cursed their way through the job, substituting the old-fashioned swear noun 'whore' (pronounced 'hoor') for any inanimate object:

"This hoor is jamming on that hoor, so if we lower together at the same time, she's gonna slide in like a good wet fuck."

My crew search was off to a dreadful start.

I had made such an effort to make Mr. and Mrs. Vance comfortable with me in their home. I had reassuring drop cloths on the stairs and comforting plastic over furniture. I tiptoed respectfully over the hardwood and I didn't play music. In less than hour, these Philistines had cussed away the working relationship that I had tried so hard to maintain with this icy couple. As I was tiptoeing out that night, Mrs. Vance loomed from the darkness at the bottom of the stairs.

"Those men who were here ... are they friends of yours?"

"Absolutely not, Mrs. Vance. I hired them for their abilities, but I could not control their language. I am sure it was upsetting to you."

I waited for a response but Mrs. Vance just kept looking at me. Finally I said:

"I apologize for bringing them into your home, and I can assure you that they will not be back."

"Ah."

"That being said, Mrs. Vance, they did good work."

"Ah."

Open Up The Wall

"Well, goodnight."

No reply. She followed me to the door, and I heard a bunch of locks click into place behind me.

I finished the job alone and uncomfortable. Whenever I looked over my shoulder, I could see the spectre of Mr. and Mrs. Vance peering at me from behind the plastic.

On my final vacuum of the place, Mr. Vance appeared at my elbow, startling me. He was wearing a tartan tie.

"Please join us in the kitchen," he said.

I followed him to the kitchen, where Mrs. Vance stood behind a table with three liqueur glasses and a single plate with three small shortbreads on it.

"I hope you can appreciate that given the state of your working clothing, we have elected to offer our thanks to you in the kitchen, rather than the living room," she said.

"Of course," I replied.

When we all had glass in hand, Mr. Vance said: "To a job well done. We are pleased. Thank you."

We drank something really sweet and Mrs. Vance said: "It's a nice deep bathtub, isn't it?"

"Room for two in there!" added Mr. Vance.

Mrs. Vance lowered her eyes and tittered, "Oh Bill!"

The best description of a joyous feeling of freedom that I have ever read is a line by Henry James – "It was June, and I was eight." I thought of it now as I shut the Vance door behind me and then raced down the street as fast as I could, for the sheer joy of it.

Hanging over me was my lack of a good crew and reliable subtrades.

My next job was the largest one that I had ever undertaken, and I would need some experienced help in order to pull it off. A producer of reality shows wanted two small sound booths with two control rooms built into his new space on the second floor of an old warehouse. He also wanted to partition off a lobby area, with a small kitchen to one side.

The space was EMPTY! All mine! I felt like I could breathe again. No drop cloths, no tiptoeing, no nightly vacuum. I could drop my tool belt in the middle of the floor at the end of the day, and pick it up from the same spot the next morning. My favourite kind of job.

The client, Jeremy, introduced me to the sound engineer who gave me beautifully detailed drawings of the two sound booths that I was to build. Then I was introduced to the designer, 'CJ', who told me of her 'concept' for the control rooms and the lobby.

For the most part, designers have little to no understanding of how things get built, so after choosing colours and fabrics most of them are out of their league when they have to talk to the contractor about practical applications. This can put them on the defensive, and that's when they get difficult to deal with.

This designer's concept for lobby partitions was a series of huge wooden boxes the size of single mattresses, perched upright on little pipe legs.

"Won't they tip over?" I asked.

CJ dressed in layers of different lengths to hide her body. Her top layer was a long wide scarf, which she tossed dramatically over her shoulder, dismissing my concern with, "That's up to you, darling."

She was right. In the end, it was up to me to make everything work out and look pretty. How much extra 'the concept' would cost the client would not be on her invoice, it would be on mine. I made sure that Jeremy was aware of this.

Open Up The Wall

There was lots of grunt work on this job so, along with a plumber and an electrician, I needed a lot of unskilled labour. The son of a friend of a friend had been calling me repeatedly, bugging me for a job. I admired his persistence, so I gave him a call.

"OK Eli, I can use you on my next job."
"Great! This is great!! When do I start?"
"Wednesday, 8:00 a.m. in the east end."
"Oh, I couldn't make it for 8:00. I live in the north end, so I'd have to get up at like, 6:00 to get there for 8:00. Wanna make it 9:30?"
"I start at 8:00."
"Ummm, OK. Thanks anyway."
???!!!???!!!???

I thought about calling Stan to see if he wanted to work with me, but I was still too uncomfortable with the way we had parted.

Little Shamus from up the street was back from university. Little Shamus had grown into a towering, muscle-bound graduate of a drama program.

"I'm looking for a job between acting gigs," he said.
"You're hired."

Shamus worked out very well. He showed up on time and he caught on quickly. I hired three young actors to manhandle the 150+ sheets of MDF and 5/8" drywall that would hang on the framing.

They got along, and they worked well together, unloading stacks of material from the trucks, and carrying it to the elevators, and then through the narrow corridors to the loft space. Apart from denting a few walls, it was a good first day.

At 8:07 a.m. on Tuesday, the first one arrived. The

second at 8:09, and the third at 8:11. They finished their coffee and went onto the fire escape for a smoke. Around 8:25 they got to work.

At 8:12 a.m. on Wednesday, they all came in together. They had met up at Starbucks and decided to finish their coffee there. Then they arrived at work and went out for a smoke.

By Friday, it was 8:20 a.m. before any of them arrived and went to the fire escape for a smoke.

At the end of the week, I handed each one of them a cheque. They stared at them. Then they compared them. Finally:

"Uh, Geoff, I think you made a mistake ... There's not enough pay here."

"You each got paid for thirty-eight-and-a-half hours work. Shamus got paid for forty hours. Did you notice him working when you arrived LATE?! EVERY SINGLE DAY?"

They were flabbergasted.

"You should have warned us! You deceived us, rather than talking to us!"

I was expecting a bit of consternation, but not such howling self-righteous anger. Nothing I said could convince them that they did not deserve to be paid for forty hours when they were only in the building for thirty-eight-and-a-half hours. They defended their position with progressively more illogical arguments.

"It's the principle of the thing!"

"Yeah! Did you take money off when we took a leak? It's the same thing!"

"Yeah! How can we trust you anymore?"

"Yeah!!! You are not reliable!!"

Open Up The Wall

Then they all stormed off to the fire escape and called their agents on me. Ten minutes later they came back and stood in a line facing me, but not looking at me. One of them announced: "We're going to give you the benefit of the doubt... So, see you on Monday."

In *Platoon*, Charlie Sheen has the line "Hell is the absence of reason."

My primary focus was still on finding skilled help. I kept hearing good things about Chris the plumber. When I found out that his company name was "Plumb It To Earth," I had to call him. His voice was so deep, rich and LOUD that I had to hold my phone away from my ear as we arranged to meet. The next afternoon, a tall lanky guy ambled in, grinned and boomed: "HI. I'M LOOKING FOR GEOFF." The four young actors came around the corner to see where such a voice was coming from.

I was so relieved to talk with a bright, like-minded individual who loved to laugh that I hired him on the spot. He became popular with everybody and — thank God — he was a brilliant plumber. He was IN!

I had known Jimmy since drama school. He had achieved fame and fortune in a number of children's series, but a costly marital breakup was now forcing him to supplement his income in the reno business, so I called him in for finish carpentry in the control rooms. It had been years since I had seen his impish face or heard his unabashed, non-stop vegetarian farting. He was IN!

Then I called Carl, an electrician. I had met him on an earlier job. He seemed to be a warm, gentle guy, so I hired him. He was great for a few days, then he stopped showing up when he said he would. That screwed up my schedule and made me mad, so on the third no-show, I called him and left a message.

"I can't rely on you, so you're fired. Get your gear out of here by 4:30."

About an hour later he stormed in and, without a word, snatched up his tool bag and advanced toward me. His mouth was open and we all eagerly awaited his parting shot. Instead, he kicked me a glancing blow to my groin, said "Fuck you, loser!" and stomped off to the elevator. All the young actors fell about laughing.

The studios were finished on time and on budget, with me working well into the night for the last two weeks. Finally all the soundproof doors were on and all the large glass panes were in the recording booths and I was worn out. The scope of the project was huge and I had done a poor job of estimating how long it would take and how much help I would need. This time however, I didn't beat myself up about it. I focused instead on all that I had accomplished, so far from my comfort zone.

One crucial thing remained to be done. I was to hang sound baffles on the walls of each booth, neatly mounted in big picture frames. The sound baffles were to be delivered in two weeks, so it was arranged that I would come back to build the twelve picture frames, install the sound baffles, and secure them to the walls.

When I called three weeks later, the recording engineer with the stupid patch of hair growing under his bottom lip, said:

"We don't need you anymore, because I put the sound baffles in myself."

"Good for you," I said. "I'll be by for my final payment."

Open Up The Wall

He had done a horrible, messy job of nailing baffles all over the walls, stapling wrinkled canvas over them, and covering the seams with strips of baseboard. Baseboard!

I asked Jeremy if the designer had endorsed this as part of her "concept." Jeremy said no, CJ had left in a huff over an unrelated matter. Then he offered me extra cash to make the walls look better.

Jeremy said he couldn't afford to take everything out and start again, so I just got rid of the baseboard and tidied up the messy walls as best I could. I said nothing about the damage to my reputation that this ugly job could potentially cost me.

I am used to homeowners who think that they can save a few bucks by putting the finishing touches on my work. When they say "I'll do the painting" or "I can put the lights up" I don't really care, but for the money saved, the end result often looks sloppy and unprofessional. If there are visible paint streaks in the new bathroom ... well, they are the ones who have to look at it. Anyway, what choice do I have?

A studio, on the other hand, can expect hundreds of people going through it every year. All of them will notice how horribly these recording booths were finished and that is ALL they will notice. Short of nailing a disclaimer to the door –THE CONTRACTOR HAD NOTHING TO DO WITH THE FINISH ON THESE WALLS – there was nothing that I could do to protect my reputation. What was particularly galling was that now the best looking part of the project was the stupid designer's stupid lobby. At least the sound designer was pleased.

"I'm getting great tone out of these rooms," he said, "and I could care less what they look like."

Oblique praise. I was still disappointed. I had thought

of bringing the family through the studios to let them see first-hand why I came home every night tired and filthy. I wanted them to understand what was so appealing about my career change, and I wanted them to be impressed with what I had done. I wanted them to be proud of me.

Instead, I left that job off my CV.

Eighteen: The Entitled

In the fall I met with Dan and Liza, a thirty-something couple who told me up front that they had received an inheritance — enough money to renovate their kitchen and expand their living area into a shed/mudroom that was on the back of their house. They took a master-servant tone with me, but luckily they both worked so I didn't see much of them.

It was a mid-sized job, and I needed an extra pair of skilled hands. The obvious choice was Stan. I wanted to work with him again, but I didn't know if the feeling would be mutual. It had been a couple of years since the Addition of Death, and even though I was calling with an offer of work, I was still anxious about re-connecting.

"Hi Stan, it's Geoff. I've got a kitchen, bathroom, and back shed conversion that I'm going to need help with. I should have all the permits next week. Anyway ... I ah ... wondered ... if you were free, if you would be interested in doing it with me?"

"Sure. Perfect timing. I'm not doing much these days. Just got back from a holiday."

Stan arrived with his tools and his Alpha personality and pretty much took control. We worked well together, dividing the jobs between us and joining forces for the heavy lifting. I had been working steadily for the two years since the Addition of Death, so our skill levels were a bit more evenly balanced now. Nonetheless, it was easy deferring to Stan's experience again, and it was a load off my mind not to be in charge of everybody and everything. I didn't lie awake at night worrying about how to deal with some tricky detail of the project, because I knew that in the morning I could get the input of a like-minded professional before deciding on a course of action. We could consult, just like other professionals.

"Hey, Stan, I'm looking under the floor and I'm not seeing much of a foundation here. Just a couple of rows of bricks. Do you think that we should delay putting the picture window in until I can give the window wall more support from underneath?"

"Yeah. This needs a lot more support."

"Can you see any way other than a new concrete foundation?"

"Sure. Put the window in, don't say anything, and then move to Guam before the whole wall sinks into the mud."

"That's a good option, because I guarantee that these yuppies are going to freak out at the extra cost. They don't get structure, they only get pretty. Damn! They will be mad at me."

"So what? They're all like that. Are you always like this?"

"Yes! As soon as I say MORE MONEY, things will change around here. No matter how I explain it, there will be a part of them that thinks I'm ripping them off .... especially these two."

"You want to be liked too much," Stan warned. "You haven't done anything wrong, so just explain the situation to them. That's the most important part of your job - making everything clear for the client. That's what they're paying you for."

"Good point. I'm so glad you're here. I mean it. Thanks."
"You're welcome. Sorry to see you're still so wussy."

When the clients arrived home that night, I explained the problem while Liza seasoned two large steaks. They tried accusing me of not anticipating the problem and hinted that we might share the extra cost.

"We're down to the hundreds of dollars now," said Dan.

I made the obvious suggestion:

"You could consider putting off some of the non-essential parts of your plan if you are struggling with the extra cost. I could hold off on building the wine cellar, for example."

As if he were talking to an idiot, Dan asked me slowly and firmly, "Then where would I put my wine?"

Liza unpacked groceries, including two bottles of Grey Goose vodka. Without warning, a famous ink drawing of Marie Antoinette flashed through my mind.

Dan and Liza were nice enough people. They worked hard, and they consumed even harder. Theirs was the generation that had been encouraged to have it all now. Going into debt for granite countertops and high-end appliances, just like the ones on reality TV, was their way of life. Like most first-time homeowners, the structural stuff is unsexy and too complicated to be of much interest to them. The trouble is, structural problems are common in older homes. For the unfortunate few who have to deal with hidden surprises, this is the time when plans and budgets get revised and compromises are made. For the Dan and Liza demographic, there is no such thing as compromise. The practical notion of saving up for something is a thing of the past. I would come to accept this as the new normal.

Stan and I carried on with expensive details — custom wall units, a coffered ceiling, an intricate series of little spice shelves to go above the $4,000 stove, and the wine cellar. We built the furniture pieces outside, on a beautiful Indian summer day, and with each piece that we brought in Dan and Liza could at last see their dream coming true in the finishing touches. And they could see the day when there would be no workmen in their perfect house.

On the second to last day, Stan was putting in baseboard and I watched him painfully get up off his knees. Finally upright, he saw me looking at him.

"Knees are the first to go," he said. "How are yours?"

"Not as bad as yours. They hurt, but they still work."

"You still walk like an old man."

"At least I don't cough like an old man."

"I have sinus problems from all the dust. I must have inhaled an entire 2X4 in my career. At least I don't wave at ... nobody."

"I'm not waving, I'm shaking my arm to loosen my shoulder. It helps my neck."

In the reflection of the big window, I saw two middle-aged men in fine physical shape. Not two decrepit old worker guys. We only felt like that.

Dan handed me a cheque for the final payment.

"It's only half," he said, "I will get the rest to you in four or five days. I hope that's OK."

In my mind, I saw myself reaching over and yanking the pointy tip of his gelled hairdo. Instead, I said: "You know that this is not what we agreed on, Dan. Situations like this have a way of getting nasty. For you, not for me."

Open Up The Wall

This was a line that I had learned from a landscaper years earlier. I had used it only a couple of times, but it seemed to work.

"Hey! I'm good for it!" Dan stammered. "It's just that I also had to put a deposit down on the cruise this week, and they didn't tell me that, so I'm short for a few days. Shit happens, right?"

All I could do was keep his house keys until he paid up.

Four days later, Dan texted that I could pick up a cheque at his office. I called and told him to courier it to me by the end of the day. He sounded surprised that I wouldn't want to leave work and drive over to his office to collect my late payment.

The thirty-somethings were a growing fascination for me, because I was getting the feeling that when it came to their renovations, they were not rooted in the reality of the situation. They just wanted it to happen and to look like the pictures when it was done. They would get angry at me if my estimate exceeded their budget, they would take calls on their cell phones in the middle of a consultation with the building inspector, that sort of thing. Nonetheless, these people were becoming a huge part of the renovation business as their parents and grandparents left them money. This group was rapidly making a name for themselves as "Spoiled Fucking Brats" or the gentler "Millennials."

My friend Manny felt the full impact of the SFBs and their sense of entitlement. After he put in a skylight for a couple who had just bought their first home, they complained that there was not enough sunlight coming through it and refused to pay him.

Manny is a small, warm-hearted Portuguese immigrant proudly helping two of his kids through medical school. He asked Jimmy and me to come and help him reason with these people.

"I don't know what more to do right for the people. Is a beautiful job, but all they can say — they won't pay."

We pulled up in front of a small house with a huge addition on the back, walked past two enormous SUVs on the parking pad, and Manny let us in through the front door.

Waiting for us at the kitchen counter at the other end of the house was a young couple, both wearing blue suits and black shoes. The man wore a tie and the woman wore high heels. There was a laptop between them. No introductions were made.

"You brought some henchmen to intimidate us, Manny?" the man said.

"We're not henchmen," I laughed, wanting to smack him already. "We're carpenters. Manny asked us to come in case there was a language issue here. He doesn't understand why you won't pay him."

The woman dramatically pecked a single key on the computer. She had sparkles on her fake nails. Up came a picture of a bathroom with a skylight with sunlight blazing through it.

"This is what we wanted," she said. "We didn't get what we wanted. It's that simple."

Manny looked around helplessly.

"I can give you a skylight, but nobody but God can give you sun," he said.

"You would have known that there wouldn't be sun,

Open Up The Wall

but you went and put the skylight in anyway! I showed you the picture Manny! It's not what I want!"

The woman was clearly upset, so I knew that this wasn't a con job for a free skylight. Nevertheless, I couldn't help laughing at her logic.

The husband looked angrily at Manny, said "just a minute" and abruptly left the room. The wife sat like a lump staring at the computer while the three of us stood in silence. Manny nervously stroked his mustache and then he said:

"Skylight! Come, I'll show you the skylight."

He took us down the hall to see his skylight job, where we stood in silence looking up at it. Jimmy said "good job" and I said "great job" and then we made faces at Manny, trying to make him laugh. Then we went back to the kitchen and looked out the window for a bit. Finally, the husband came back with a chequebook and spoke quietly to his wife.

"I called Dad and he says we don't have a leg to stand on, so we have to pay him."

The woman looked straight at Manny and said: "Oh, my God! This is SO not fair!"

Poor Manny was cheated out of the recognition of a job well done. "Is a beautiful job," he said to the woman. "No leaks ... ever."

"This is SO not fair!"

The husband put a cheque on the counter, glared at Manny again, and left the room. The woman stared at the computer, breathing heavily. Manny told her he was upset that she wasn't happy, but she ignored us and began tapping away on her laptop, so we left.

I couldn't put my finger on why this episode was so

unnerving. As tradesmen, we were all used to being treated like third-class citizens, so it wasn't that. It was more that I was seeing the adjustment that I would have to make in the way that I did business with a segment of the population. Now I had to contend with a demographic that was used to having everything made alright for them. I had to come face to face with people who spent their formative years playing non-competitive board games at Montessori schools. As Manny had found out, they can turn nasty if their demands are not met, no matter what the circumstances. I had to figure out a way to have a creative, constructive business relationship with people who grew up being told that they were special — the ones who got achievement ribbons for EVERYTHING THEY EVER DID.

For different groups, I have different 'Rules of Engagement'. For families where language might be an issue, I draw pictures of the job, with prices beside them. For some cultures, I make sure to address the men only and never even glance at any women present. For contemporary yuppies, I make sure to make equal eye contact with both sexes. For older people, I follow up on the initial meeting with a phone call a couple of days later, because I know that they will be feeling overwhelmed with reno information.

These were the brief, simple rules that I had come up with over the years to keep everybody calm and comfortable with the renovation experience.

The first rule for The Entitled would be ... patience:

"I know the paint matches the sample! I know it looks the same, but I SAY IT IS DIFFERENT! Jesus Christ! What is the matter with you!?"

Nineteen: Know When to Fold 'Em

If there is a sensual side to the renovation business, it is working with wood. Not the coarse spruce framing lumber with a smell that attracts wasps, but the oak, pine, and poplar from which we build cabinets and bookshelves. These are smooth to the touch, with a calming scent, and if you take the time to look, you can get lost in the details of their flowing grain. I don't get to work with real wood that much anymore, now that laminates and fibreboards have become the industry standard, so when a lady called about laying a pine floor in her bedroom, I moved her to the top of the list. Working with the fragrant softwood was a dream job, a pleasant respite from bathrooms and basements, pipes, and jackhammers. I wanted to do it alone, and in silence, thus creating a soothing interlude for my mind, body, and soul.

From my vast array of tools, all I took to this job was a tape measure, a pencil, a speed square, and a manual floor nailer. These were the only tools that I owned when I laid my first pine floor so many years ago. And my Skil saw. I brought my Skil saw, my second one since the first one that had frightened me so much. This one was a larger, more solid, matronly saw, the Skil-Mag77. She had been with me for twelve years now and of all my tools I cherished her the most, having held her in my hands most days of my life. I kept her well oiled, and she never let me down. I could see our history together in her well-worn blade guard, the progression of our growth in the reno business with every scratch and dent in her body. If she ever burns out I will have to put her on a shelf somewhere, carefully wrapped up in something significant. After all that we have accomplished together, it wouldn't be right to just throw her away.

After I hit the last tongue into the last groove with a satisfying smack, I lay face down on the wood and breathed through my nose. The smell of pine will always trigger memories of my first floor, and my first encounter with a power tool so many years, and so many jobs ago.

Lying on the pine, I had one of those wonderful moments of seeing the people and events in my life from a completely different perspective – like when your dog enters the room and you become hyper aware that you share your dwelling with another species. It was easy to see myself as one of the lucky ones – those who are loosely in control of their destiny, but the shocking part was the clarity with which I saw that personal freedom was something to be protected. Of course, everybody who is self-employed, already knows that.

It has taken me a long time to put my sense of self worth ahead of making money. In fact, it's a constant battle, forcing myself to trust the voice in my head that says: "You are walking into a quagmire of mistrust and resentment that no amount of money will make worthwhile. Get Out Now!"

Penny the realtor called me with a typical set of circumstances – her baby boomer clients are now

Open Up The Wall

empty nesters, and they are going to sell the family home. They want way more than the house is worth, because nothing has been done to the place since they moved in 30 years ago.

"I can't guarantee that they will follow through on any of my suggestions," said Penny. "They're quite...um...high maintenance...but they've agreed to have you come and price a new kitchen. They're having a life crisis about dipping into their nest egg."

"How old are they?"

"Kinda your age... kinda hippie era...I thought you would be a good fit for them."

"...Thanks."

The house was in the Birkenstock part of town, where bearded college professors chain their bikes to the porches of their Victorian homes. I stepped over a FOR SALE sign face down on the front porch. "Boomers in transition" I thought to myself. "Going through hell parting with the family home, pulling the house off the market in tears, and then putting it back on in tears."

The antique brass door ringer didn't work, so I knocked on the refinished pine door. A dream catcher moved in the door's window, and a bearded face appeared in its place. The man looked me up and down before opening the door.

All he said was "Yes?"

I identified myself, and handed him my card. He barely looked at it before thrusting it into the pocket of his striped cardigan.

"So you're the big expert are you?" asked the man. Then he laughed as if to indicate that his remark was really a joke.

"I'm here to see if I can help." I said.

"For a price, of course." And he laughed that laugh again.

In the face of such a remark, I abandoned pleasantries and stood watching the wind chimes on the porch until he got uncomfortable.

"Wait while I get my wife."

Leaving me outside, the man headed down the hall. A skinny Siamese cat came from the kitchen, froze when it saw me, and let out that awful Siamese cat yowl that passes for a meow.

"DON'T LET THE CAT OUT!" Screamed a woman's voice, and the cat yowled again.

The man scurried back, scooped up the noisy pet, and stood beside me in the open doorway as a tall woman in a long skirt came clinking down the stairs. Only when she snatched the cat from the man, did I see that the clinking sound came from a collection of bracelets on her right arm.

"And you are?" She demanded.

"I'm the contractor who has the 5 PM appointment with Mr. and Mrs. Stibbard."

"Well we're the Stibbards, obviously."

"Nice to meet you." I lied. "I'm Geoff. Your husband has my card."

Mr. gave Mrs.the card,who tossed it onto the hall table without looking at it.

Mrs. Stibbard said "And you're going to try to sell us a new kitchen."

"Or so Penny thinks anyway." Said Mr. Stibbard, and laughed the 'sorry I was born' laugh again.

Penny is young and beautiful, which can be construed as inexperienced and flighty by some of her

Open Up The Wall

clients. That's when she calls me, Old Worker Guy, to back her up. If Penny can get a mistrustful client to understand the importance of home upgrades in a competitive real estate market, and if I can give them a dollar amount that will work with their budget, then everyone can remain calm and profit from the very trying process of selling a beloved home. We don't have to like each other, we just have to get along for a little while.

I was having my own kind of trouble getting along with the Stibbards. For me, it is disheartening to see people of the Woodstock generation forget where they came from, and turn greedy and unkind, so when I saw the kitchen that they were insisting was just fine as it was, I spoke more candidly than diplomatically.

"Penny is right." I said.This kitchen looks dirty. Even if it had just been scrubbed clean,it is so worn that it still looks grungy. Also, I can see water damage to the counter under the HOT tap. And the smell of incense in here is probably masking a smell of mildew."

Mrs.Stibbard fixed her gaze on me and nodded her head vigorously, making her dangling earrings tinkle.

"That's what Penny said! Exactly what Penny said!"

"J'accuse!" Said Mr. Stibbard, and laughed the sorry laugh.

Mrs. Stibbard pushed the cat at Mr. Stibbard and said "Shut up Tick!" Then, in a somewhat threatening way for a woman of her age, she moved very close to my face, and said:

"This is a serious question, and I want a serious answer out of you: what is your involvement in this real estate deal?"

"I'm not used to being talked to like that." I said, taking a step back. "But because of my involvement with Penny, I will explain the situation."

"Oh my God!" Cried Mr. Stibbard. "You're involved with Penny?!?"

"SHUT UP TICK!" shouted Mrs. Stibbard. The cat yowled again from Mr. Stibbard's arms.

"STOP SHOUTING" shouted Mr. Stibbard. "You made Ringo scratch me."

"Oh for Christ's sake Tick! I'm trying to get to the bottom of this!"

Mr. Stibbard put down the cat and shot back: "So am I! You think I don't have questions too?" He did his laugh again.

"What are you talking about? You have shown absolutely NO interest in getting us out of here! I have done EVERYTHING!"

"YES! YES! Because you just take over!"

That was my cue. "I'll be outside." I said. "I have to make a call..."

"Stay there!" Panted Mrs. Stibbard. "My husband has some questions for you. Go ahead and ask your questions Tick! You have questions, so ASK THEM! Was it something about the moving company? because I've already organized EVERYTHING! Was it about the legal and land transfer? Because I've already organized EVERYTHING!"

"What? This is my house."

"Oh yes, I moved into YOUR HOUSE and I took care of EVERYTHING for TWENTY SEVEN YEARS!! OK FINE! THIS IS YOUR HOUSE! NOW SHUT UP!!"

The woman was gasping for breath, the cat would not shut up, and 'Tick' was looking frightened. With her

Open Up The Wall

chest heaving inches from my own, she panted:
" I want to know your involvement in this house sale! You are obviously the one to benefit from Penny's scheme to make us build a new kitchen, and I think there's a scam at work here! Am I right? How does it work? Do you split the take with Penny?"

I was more alarmed by the woman's laboured breathing than I was by her accusation.

"I can call the police you know!"

Tick moved towards his wife. "Amber" he said "soften, soften..."

"I WILL NOT! CAN'T YOU SEE WHAT'S GOING ON HERE? YOU DON'T KNOW ANYTHING!"

Of the myriad weird situations that a tradesman encounters when meeting people in their homes, watching a couple yell at each other face to face, is probably the most unneving. Typically, a couple will excuse themselves from the room, and I listen to a whispered argument full of sharp consonants:

"KeeP your voiCE Down!"

"Then SToP being So STupid!"

As long as they aren't discussing me, I find the 'whisperers' quite amusing. But I'm uncomfortable with the 'eye rollers' who react to their partner's ideas by looking at me and rolling their eyes. Even harder to take are the 'signers' who will slip behind their partner to wave at me, mouthing 'NO' or mime slitting their throat. If the eyes are the window to the soul, surely somebody in the room can see how troubled my soul is, watching a person devalue their partner, while I stand passively by.

When Mrs.Stibbard's breathing had returned to normal, I said "If you don't want a new kitchen, you don't have to have one. Penny will simply list your house as a 'fixer upper' and it will sell for less than the upgraded homes on your street. I am only here to give you a price on how much the recommended upgrades to your house would cost. Penny would then discuss with you if such a renovation investment would have a profitable return. At this point, there are no costs involved."

"Oh."

"Oh. (sorry laugh)"

"However, you have such resistance to this whole idea, that I see no point in wasting all our time by continuing with an estimate."

"Oh."

"Oh. (sorry laugh)"

"Good luck with the sale." I said from the hall table, where I made a show of retrieving my card, and putting it back in my wallet before walking to the door. Mrs. Stibbard followed and as she shut the door behind me, she said in a too loud voice: "What a horrible man."

Penny was anxious that I had jeopardized her listing, until I bet her $100.00 that the Stibbards would never go for a new kitchen. My certainty seemed to reassure her, but being young and ambitious, she had trouble with the notion of turning down a job.

"The jobs come and go," I said, "so why would I choose to spend a couple of weeks enduring the anxiety and resentment of creepy people like the Stibbards when I don't actually need to?"

"C'mon – we all put up with clients we don't like as people. This is business, it's part of the job."

"Yeah, but I don't handle that kind of dismissive disrespect too well anymore. As you will find out, my young

Open Up The Wall

colleague, it gets harder to take, until one day, one job, one client, the cost is too great and you have to take your life back. By the way, Mr. Stibbard thinks we're 'involved'. I said something about my involvement with you, and he took it to mean 'involved' involved."

"Eew!"

"You might want to clear that up."

" No doubt!"

The Stibbards had more or less invited me to reject them. Sometimes the decision to walk away comes flying from my gut before I can even call it an informed decision:

The cockney on the phone wanted a price on taking out a wall, and I had to agree to be at his house at precisely 9:55 AM.

At the appointed time, I pulled into the driveway of a ranch style home, and a muscular man of about 60 leapt off the porch and hurried over to the truck. There was a tattoo of a scaly serpent on his chest, holding an arrow in its mouth, and some trees. On his belt was a long commando style knife.

"Geoff I presume?"

"Yes. You must be Gerald."

"Yes indeed. Now listen mate, my wife has a grand design, but my budget is not as grand ... so ... anything you can do to help me out ... yeah?"

"... I'm not sure I understand ..."

"Just follow my lead. The lads stick together, yeah?"

Gerald ushered me through the front door with an elaborate sweeping somehow bow, as a number of clocks chimed 10.

"Geoff, may I introduce my wife Charlotte?" announced Gerald, as a pretty woman with a long braid of silver grey hair approached. She wore a sleeveless floor length dress, and I saw a strand of barbed wire tattooed around her left arm, not far from her unshaven underarm.

"Welcome Geoff." she said. "Now I hope you can do open concept, because that's what I'm after ..."

"If it is even possible ..." snorted Gerald, looking at me conspiratorially.

"I think that it will be nice to be able to look into the living room from the kitchen" continued Charlotte. "So let's hear what the man has to say, love."

She gave him a warm, kind smile.

"You have a couple of options," I said, "but the important thing for you to know is that this is a bearing wall, so if I take it away, something has to replace it, to hold up the floor above. This will necessitate a beam across the ceiling where the wall was, held up by posts on either side, which go all the way down to the basement and rest on footings, which are two deep, wide holes jackhammered through the concrete floor in the basement, and filled with concrete."

"This sounds bloody expensive!"

"Gerald!"

"Yes it is." I said. "I've described the scope of work very generally, to give you an idea of the dirt, and noise, and upheaval that you will have to put up with, but also, so you can see that it isn't as simple as just sawing the wall away. It will take about a week to complete, and it will cost between five and six thousand dollars, depending on how much wire and pipe must be re-routed, and how you choose to dress the beam, the walls, and the floor where the old wall was."

Nobody spoke for a bit. Gerald and Charlotte looked at each other – warmly, I thought, but Gerald's

Open Up The Wall

hand rested on the hilt of his knife.

I broke the silence. "A cheaper option would be to cut an opening in the existing wall..."

"No no! Six grand is great!" Beamed Charlotte. "I was thinking around ten or fifteen grand. We can do this Gerald!"

Gerald began marching in a wide circle around the living room, swinging his arms like a soldier on a parade square.

"Six grand is a trip to Italy! Six grand is a bleeding month in Mexico! Six grand gets us flights to Australia!"

Charlotte was clearly embarrassed, and I was getting nervous, afraid that the knife might be featured in his performance.

"Why are you changing your tune now Gerald?"

"Because it's six bleeding grand!!"

"We can't travel forever darling, and I want the house to look nice..."

Gerald glared at me and shouted "Thanks mate!" and marched away, down a hall to what I assumed was an exercise room, because I heard the clanging of iron bars, and loud exhalations.

"When would you be able to start?" Charlotte asked.

"...Um, early April." I said. "But I'm reluctant to proceed with a detailed estimate for you, when your husband is clearly opposed to the idea."

"My husband is none of your concern!" Snapped Charlotte, as if insulted.

"Well, in a way he is." I countered. "There are a lot of decisions that have to be made between the three of us if you want this small renovation to happen on time, and on budget. In fact, there are usually about 25 things that we all have to agree on. Now, if your husband needs more time to come around to the idea, I would be happy to provide a scale drawing of the proposed changes, so that you two could work out the details together. I mean, it's better that a renovation be an undertaking that brings you closer together, than one that pits you against each other. There is no joy in that..."

Charlotte raised both arms above her head, locking her fingers together in an apparent gesture of frustration, because she said:

"Oh for Christ's sake! Enough of this airy-fairy psychobabble! Do you want the job or not?"

My mind and my mouth responded by reflex – the way ones hand will fly up to protect ones face when a dangerous object comes too close.

"No." I said. "I don't want the job."

"What?!? Bloody hell! No??"

From down the hall Gerald called "Don't give that bloke any money!"

Turning down work is a calculated risk. If nothing comes up to fill that time slot, there will be a few of us out of work. It's hard to explain to a crew that was counting on a job that I turned it down because 'it didn't feel right'. My biggest fear in a situation like this is that they will get work from someone else, and it will be hard for me to get them back into the fold.

Twenty: The Addition of Life

In June, Stan called.

"I have an addition for the summer."
"What kind?"
"Third storey. Close by. Nice people. You want to do it with me?"

Building a brand new structure of this size and scope, outdoors in the summer, would be a really cool job. The added bonus of building a third floor is that there would be no clients around.

But The Addition of Death flashed before my eyes. Access to a 3rd floor addition is by ladder until the hole gets cut in the roof to put in the stairs. Everything goes up by ladder. Lumber, concrete block, attitude, and anxiety all get piled on the roof. You have to watch your step.

I went around to look at the site before I said yes. Sure enough, there was the ladder.

"I can't move my legs," it said.

Stan had secured the ladder perpendicular to the wall. I ascended with purpose, feeling fear ooze into my joints and make me doubt my every move.

It was a flat roof. No peaks or hips to slide off and fall to my death three stories below, except for one. Just one really steep pitch at the front of the house, running its entire width. Not scary enough to pass on such a great job, especially since I had learned about safety harnesses after working on The Addition of Death. I would simply get the best safety harness that money could buy.

When descending a ladder, it is important to look up. This keeps the body closer to the ladder. Never look at your feet. If you look down on the descent, you force your body away from the ladder and put more stress on your hands, which could slip, and, with your body so far away from the ladder, you would not recover balance in time to save yourself from falling and smashing your head like a melon on the ground below. I looked up so intently that I could hear my belt buckle scraping the ladder all the way down.

"People who have had a height scare often get a tingling in their crotch when next they attempt a high climb," said the ladder. "So how's your weenie feeling today?"

"Well, it's tingling," I said, "but not enough to scare me off. Now get out of my head."

I called Stan and said, "I'm in."

Three of us started the demolition on one of the hottest July days on record. Me, Stan, and Ian, a voice actor. On this job, Ian would come and go as his schedule permitted.

Our first task was to build a big slide, forty feet long and four feet wide. It reached from the roof, down to the backyard lawn. This slide would convey the demolition debris down, and the new lumber up.

Next we had to get rid of the existing tar-and-gravel flat roof so that we could put in thicker joists and turn the 2nd floor ceiling into a floor. We cut the old roof out in chunks and pitched them onto our slide. Our

Open Up The Wall

saws begged for mercy as we forced their blades through dense tar-soaked membrane embedded with gravel.

One after the other, we pitched the worn, tarred blades off the roof until the lawn below was littered with them — glinting in the sunlight like an aerial view of a convoy of ships.

By five o'clock, the last piece of the toxic goo got pitched down our slide, and we were straddling the joists, looking down at the ceilings below. No rain was forecast, but after the disaster at the Addition of Death, Stan was taking no chances, so we covered the house with layers and layers of tarps.

We worked out a tie-down method that would not only protect our work, but also keep any rain from going into the other half of the semi-detached home. With huge tarps, we made the flat roof up like a bed, hospital corners and all. When we were satisfied that it was impermeable, we climbed down the ladder and I headed for my truck, with a happy thought of me cozying up to a beer in the shower and watching the black tarry residue drip off my body. In the backyard, Ian washed himself down with a hose and then put on clean clothes. I assumed that he couldn't get to a shower before a dinner engagement or something.

The next morning, Ian arrived in a linen shirt, slacks, and sandals.

"Looks like you have an audition today," I said.

"No."

"Then why are you dressed so well?"

"No reason. I've got my work clothes in my backpack."

Ian was ashamed to be seen as a common workman,

so every night he washed up under the hose and changed clothes for the subway ride home. In his heart, he was just passing through the filthy world that I was so proud to be part of.

Stan had things well planned out and the existing roof structure gave us no surprises. Everything seemed to fall into place on time and on budget. Away from everybody, surrounded by sky and treetops, we could easily slip into 'The Zone' and work together for hours in Zen-like industry before the heat drove us down the ladder for water and shade. Ian had taken to bringing sliced limes and stuffing them into the fifteen bottles of water that the three of us were downing every day.

On the afternoon that Stan and I finished gluing and screwing the subfloor down, our backs were killing us, so we lay on the new plywood, looking up at big cumulus clouds. The stink of the tar was gone, replaced by the perfumey smell of cut plywood. A breeze passed over our sweat-soaked T-shirts, cooling us down. We lay listening to a cardinal singing from the trees below us. This was job satisfaction as I had never known it before. After a while, Stan said:

"We should remember this moment."

I don't know which one woke me, the crash of the thunder or the bedside phone ringing in my ear, but in a total panic I leapt out of bed, ran downstairs and answered the phone in the kitchen.

"What's going on? Yes? Hello?"

"Can you get over here right away?"

In an instant I was wide awake.

"Oh fuck."

"Disaster."

Open Up The Wall

"On my way."

I ran back upstairs and felt around in the dark for my work clothes, which sit in a pile behind the laundry hamper until they get dirty enough to go IN the laundry hamper. In less time than it takes to feed a cat, I was dressed and driving to the site with my windshield wipers on HIGH.

I went straight to the front door. All the lights were on, so I walked in. Stan's ashen face appeared in the hallway.

"The rain has got into the other side of the semi. The last time this happened at the addition at Martin's ..."

"Yeah, I remember. The rain ruined the hardwood floor."

We went next door to the other side of the semi-detached home and met Marlene and Richard, the owners. They showed me their bathroom, with quite a big wet spot on the ceiling, and a bowl on the floor, half full of water.

I almost laughed out loud. "That's IT?" I asked.

"Isn't that enough?" brayed Richard. "The whole ceiling is soaked!"

Stan was taking deep breaths, so I said: "OK, we'll have a look outside and be right back."

With the door shut behind us, I said, "Stan! There's no disaster here! There is just a wet ceiling. The damage here we can fix in three days."

"We have to find the leak!" replied Stan. "Jesus! It hasn't rained like this since the last time I did an addition."

"I know. I was there. This time it's going to be OK."

We went up on the roof, and went over the tarps with flashlights, until we found a 3-inch tear and a trickle of water heading towards the other side of the semi. We taped up the tear and then we went home.

As long as I could hear the rain on my roof, I couldn't sleep. Neither could Stan. He was on the phone to his insurance company first thing the next morning. Then he spent half an hour assuring Marlene and Richard that an entirely new bathroom ceiling would be installed and painted at no cost to them.

Later, they tried to scam a whole new bathroom out of him.

Ian and I began pushing the lumber up our slide for the walls and roof of the new addition. Three-quarters of the roof space would be the new rooms, while the remaining quarter would be a walkout deck.

"I'm going to the 'Indy 500' for three days next week," announced Stan, "so I want to get everything framed in before I go."

The walls went up easily. Now came the scary part. We had to climb on the top of the walls, and walk along the 5½" wide top plate, while we laid out the ceiling joists every 16" without falling three storeys to the pavement below.

It was really high and really windy. One good gust … it had Addition of Death written all over it.

But this time I was prepared!

I said dramatically: "Just let me get into my safety harness."

Stan jumped up. "What? You got a safety rig? Lemme see that thing!"

I pulled the rig out of its orange carry bag. Stan took

Open Up The Wall

the harness and stepped into it.

"I'll go first!"

Ian and I tightened all the straps, and I clipped the safety rope to the steel ring on the back of the harness. I was reading the instruction paragraph "Securing The Safety Rope" when I heard a shout from Stan.

"Oh yeah! No fear up here anymore!! Good call buying this thing!"

He was walking along the edge of the narrow ridge beam on the scary pitch of the roof.

I surprised myself with a near falsetto scream. "Stan! Stop! Don't move!"

"I am invincible!"

"You're not attached!"

When he saw me standing with the other end of the safety rope in my hand he froze and then dropped, painfully straddling the ridge beam, legs dangling in the air below.

"Tie me off! Tie me off! Oh God, my nuts ..."

I clipped the rope to the cast-iron toilet stack sticking up out of the deck.

"OK, you're good."

Down he came, holding his groin, but with a grin on his face. All he said was, "This thing ROCKS!"

I never got to wear my harness on that job. Stan took it over and clambered all over the scary side of the house while I worked where I could only fall eight feet.

By Friday, we had the addition framed and we had pushed twelve sheets of 4'X8' plywood sheathing up our slide. On Monday, we would cover the frame. The design was for a flat roof and, at this stage the frame was open to the elements, with the exposed ceiling joists resembling a pergola. Light showers were forecast for Saturday, so we laid tarps across the ceiling joists, and secured them from another wind tear. Great progress, and nobody fell to their death. The worst was over. Stan left for the Indy 500.

The showers grew more intense and by Saturday evening there was a big wind, so I went over to check the tarps. They were intact, but the rain was collecting in the spaces between the joists, causing the tarp to sag under the weight. I took a push broom, and pushed it up under each space, forcing the water to flow from the sagging tarps and off the sides of the house. Then I went home. The rain did not stop, so I came back at 10:00 p.m. and repeated the process, and then I went to bed. I woke to heavy rain on my roof at 2:30 a.m. so I went back to do the routine again. Ho-hum.

I drove down the laneway at the back of the house and parked in my usual spot facing the ladder.

Wearing my miner's light on my forehead, I began the climb up the ladder. Nearing the top, I felt an intense beam of light on me and I could sense flashing lights below. I didn't know what was going on, but I wanted to get off the ladder ASAP, so I continued climbing in the rain. A bullhorn crackled, and a woman's voice said:

"Police! Come down here!"

The bright light following me as I slowly made my way to the ground.

"Put your hands where I can see them, and walk towards the vehicle ... WALK!"

I shot my arms in the air and walked to the police car with the red lights flashing.

Open Up The Wall

"I'm not a robber," I said. "I work here."
"At 3:12 a.m.?"
"Yes. It's an emergency."
The officer shoved me to the front of the cruiser, where I was lit by the headlights.
"Put your hands on the hood!"
She took my wallet from my back pocket and then felt all around the waistband of my pants, which was strangely arousing.
"Pretty strange to come to work on a rainy night without rain gear, isn't it?"
"I'm only here to prevent a disaster, then I'm going back to bed."
"OK," she said, "you can turn around. Now, what's going on?"
When I turned around, I faced a young lady who looked much too slight and vulnerable for her job, and I briefly worried about her. Then I refocused, and explained the situation:
"Up there is the frame of a third floor with no roof covering it yet. There is only a tarp draped over the top, over the ceiling joists. The rain is collecting in the gaps between those joists. If I don't push the water out of the gaps from below, the tarp will tear and that water could find its way into the house."
The officer shone her floodlight on the sagging tarp.
"Jeepers!" she said. "You better get up there!"
I climbed back up the ladder, this time with the officer's great beam of light following me. What a sweetheart. On my way up the ladder I tried to remember her face.
When I got to the roof I waved at the light and

called "Thank You" in a stage whisper. Then I turned my headlamp on, got my broom, and began to push water over the side of the house. On the ground, the officer stood in the rain, now in her rain gear, and followed me with her beam for about ten minutes until I had pushed all the water away and climbed back down the ladder to the cruiser.

"Thanks for your help," I said. "That was so kind of you."

"No problem," she said. "Stay safe. Toodaloo."

She got into her cruiser and drove into the night alone, and I worried for her all over again.

I told the whole story to Stan when he returned on Tuesday. I mentioned the frisking, and he demanded details:

"Was it just the physical frisking, or was it being frisked by a girl in a uniform and wearing a gun that turned you on?"

"Wait! I didn't say I was turned on!"

"Not in so many words...but I'll bet you own a pair of handcuffs."

At 10:30 we climbed down for some water with lime wedges. In the kitchen were four women also having water and lime after their tennis doubles. They greeted us cordially, asked how things were going and within thirty seconds they were making remarks about men in tool belts. These professional women egged each other on to moan and sigh while they joked about sweaty workmen and rough hands. It was all in good fun but it made us uncomfortable, so we sliced our limes, and got out of the kitchen quickly. It's OK for women to make sexual comments about men, but the

Open Up The Wall

reverse is more likely to have consequences. Renovators in particular must be aware of this, spending so much time as they do with the lady of the house.

"It's their revenge for all the whistles and catcalls they put up with from construction workers," Ian said from the safety of our rooftop.

"We ARE construction workers," I said.

As soon as we finished sheathing the frame in plywood, Stan immediately called the roofers.

The next afternoon, up the ladder, carrying heavy rolls of roofing membrane, came three NICE ROOFERS. They were a far cry from the Neanderthals on the studio job so many years earlier. We helped out where we could, stayed out of the way when we should, and five hours later they were done. Stan bought everybody beer.

Finally high and dry, we started on the inside. We cut the opening for the stairs to the third floor and put temporary stairs in on the second floor for the plumbers, electricians and HVAC guys to access the site with all their gear. As the family was still living in the house, we continued to use our ladder on the outside wall, just to keep the disruption to a minimum. I suddenly realized that I was up and down those worn rails all day long with never a fear of falling to my death, and the ladder was not talking to me anymore. The curse of The Addition of Death had lifted.

On the afternoon that I finished the mantle over the master bedroom fireplace, I went over to look at the custom shower that Stan had built and was now tiling. It was gorgeous in its detail.

I said, "How is it that you can be an actor in the most

mindless teen slasher movie and people call you an artist, but when you design and build something like this shower, this work of art, you're just an old worker guy?"

"Makes no sense," said Stan. He wasn't listening. He was focused on cutting expensive Italian tile.

But Paul heard me. I had forgotten that he was in the stairwell, putting in the ductless air conditioning. Tiny perfect Paul, who always wore the tradesman stay-press blue pants and matching shirt with a badge that read "PAUL." His hair shone with some product that made it immovable, but still collected dust.

"Wait! What? Are you saying that you're actors? Seriously? Why on earth would you want to do that?"

The long silence told me that Stan was not going to run with this question, so I did. "Because," I said, "Stan is a child of alcoholic parents and I was abandoned at birth, so we need more approval than most people do. When we perform in plays, and people clap for us, we feel validated."

It was sort of cruel of me to send up Paul in this way, but sort of worth it. He turned around twice in his tracks, smacking a plastic water bottle against his thigh, clearly disturbed by this revelation.

"Are you guys saying you are actors posing as contractors?"

"No, not at all. This is what we do now. We're licensed."

"Well, OK then. I mean ... you seem like normal guys."

Forty minutes later Paul finished and came up from the stairwell. Stan signed his work order and we made our goodbyes. Paul lingered at the top of the stairs before he

Open Up The Wall

posed probably the weirdest question ever put to me:
"This acting thing – does it have something to do with getting laid?"

The last of the custom stuff arrived — chandeliers, closet doors, and keyless locks. By the end of the day it would all be finished. We walked through bedroom with the fireplace, past the bathroom with the walk-in shower and out to the cedar deck, where we unscrewed our slide and our access ladder and pushed them off the house to the ground below.

"I'll be sorry to leave this one," I said. "It's a beautiful job and it was good time."

"We should start a company together," Stan said, "and just do additions."

This was a surprise. "I'm touched that you would want to partner with me."

"Don't cry. You have to be the front man. I need a large break from dealing with clients."

He began imitating a whining homeowner: "Stan, can you shave down the price a bit? I've given you lots of work over the years ..."

"I get that too," I said.

"Yeah? Do you get this: "Hey Pal, why don't you bring the family up to our cottage this weekend. The weather is going to be great, and I got a new barbeque. Oh, and I got a new water pump for the place, so if you bring your plumbing tools you can hook that sucker up and then I'll get some steaks going."

"That's cruel."

"I'm afraid of getting invitations now. I keep waiting for the catch."

Stan went off to put counters in a bike shop, and I

took Shamus to help me gut a house.

Then I got an email from Gene and Lydia with attached drawings for a ground-floor addition. They wanted to remodel their existing house with a new bathroom, new kitchen, and laminate flooring throughout. Then they wanted a 14'X20' family room on the back. This was perfect. Stan and I could get going on his idea of our addition company.

I forwarded the email to Stan with the note, "This looks promising."

No reply for three days. On Saturday morning he called me.

"There's no point in us doing this addition together. There's not enough money in it for both of us."

"Of course there is! There are four weeks of interior renovation before we even get to the addition. What are you telling me? I thought that this was what you wanted to do?"

He was rambling and obtuse, seizing on the catch phrase "It's all about the money." With no logical explanation forthcoming, I gave up.

"OK. I'll do it without you."

That was the last I saw of Stan for two years. Again.

Twenty-One: The Addition of Discovery

I was pretty sure I could handle it. I had done additions before, but never as the sole bearer of responsibility for everything that could go wrong. For all the various trucks pulling up on the sidewalk of the residential street. For the moving of bricks and lumber by crane into the backyard. For having to hire a cop by the day to stand around and police these goings-on. For the dumpster's street permit and the dumpster security, so that neighbours don't fill it up with old couches when we go for lunch. For the flow of money from client to worker, from general contractor (me) to Worker's Comp. For the "Call Before You Dig" application. For safety equipment for everybody on site. For the complete cleanup every night, so that nobody can trip over anything and sue us. For the diplomatic dealing with neighbour complaints of dust and noise. For the diplomatic dealing with the building inspectors, and the architect and the building inspector's complaints about the architect's drawings.

I felt an anxiety that I hadn't felt since my first studio job, so many years ago. Back then, it came from starting every day not knowing what was going to happen next. Now, it came from seeing the immediate future and knowing that it was up to me to control everything that was going to happen next, every day for weeks and weeks. I could feel the sleepless nights ahead, but I was also excited by the challenge. Look at me now Ma — I am now the BOSS of a whole bunch of common tradesmen!

I had a stellar crew for the inside of the house. Shamus was in for gutting the bathroom and kitchen. I lined up Chris the plumber for the new bathroom and kitchen, and Jimmy was going to do the tiling and had also promised to do any of the picky, detailed stuff that I hated doing. The new guys were Rico the electrician, who crowed regularly about how happy he was to be out of Cuba, and Phil, who I had hired to help with flooring and cabinetry but ended up becoming my right-hand man, he was so organized and competent. Phil had multi skills from working on his own houses, so when he retired early as a high school VP, I snapped him up.

They were all family men, which meant that they could be counted on to not show up hungover, and not spend the day on their phones. They were all well read and witty, which made for great lunchtime discussions, and they all had good manners. Manners were important, as this house was packed in between two others, with a narrow 32" walkway on one side as the only separation. Good relations with the neighbours and their children would be critical, given what they were about to endure for a couple of months.

The clients, Gene and Lydia, had rented an apartment for the duration, so the day their family moved out Phil and I got started removing an unused chimney that was taking up space inside the two-storey house. I straddled the peak of the roof and began pitching bricks into the back yard, while Phil piled them against the fence.

I heard somebody bellow: "What the hell you? Why you doing my fence damage?"

Open Up The Wall

Great. Day One, and I have a neighbour issue. They are rarely serious, it's usually just humans guarding their territory, but diplomacy is paramount. I climbed down to see a big old man leaning over the fence, with his large head poking between two downspouts that were running from his house, duct-taped to the fence and slathered in a clear, gelatinous goo.

I introduced Phil and myself, gave him my card and explained the work that we would be doing. We stood in silence while he studied my card intently. When I complemented him on his waterproof downspouts, he looked up proudly.

"Lot of work. Lot of rubber cement. Last forever!"

Sure enough, the goo was dry. It was indeed rubber cement.

"Come on boys, I show you."

He led us on a tour of his yard showing us posts, stairs, watering cans and a bicycle seat, all duct taped and covered in rubber cement. Then he led us to his workshed, where he presented me with two Skil saw blades from a pile of about twenty.

"A gift from me. I am Frank."

"You're very kind Frank," I said.

"I give you more stuff later. Now, I go lie down, so don't you make big noises. Later I come and see what you and you are doing over there."

The next day was the official Day One of the Full House Reno. The day that the workspace is emptied of the client's furniture and personal effects. All that stuff gets wrapped in plastic. Then all the tools gets carried in and arranged — the table saw in the longest room for ripping the longest lengths, mitre saw to one side. The other side is where all the lumber gets stacked. Hand tools, tool bags, first aid kit, brooms, and vacuum get lined up in one room, and hardware in another — new sinks, toilets, bathtubs, boxes of tile, boxes of screws, garbage bags, etc. etc.

Day One is usually the first time that the contractor has been in the space since making the deal with the homeowner, which could have been weeks earlier. I took my notes and walked through the beautiful old house, refreshing my memory as to all that was going to happen.

A lot of the work on this house would involve taking out the ninety-year-old trim and baseboards, restoring them to their past glory, and reinstalling them. For all of the trades involved, this is a much more satisfying way to work than just throwing up pot lights and a granite counter top and calling it renovated. Gene and Lydia wanted to keep the essence of the place, with its wide baseboard, ornate door and window trim, plaster mouldings, and ceiling medallions. These people wanted the history of this house to survive the renovation right down to the porcelain doorknobs. They were spending their money on repairing the stained glass above the doors, instead of putting a heated floor in the bathroom. The banisters were going to be refinished, not torn out. When I put my hand on the side of the top post, which was rubbed free of its varnish and lacquer, I could feel all the years of children's hands gripping the post as they swung a leg up and slid down the long banister. All the cuts and splinters that I was going to get on this job, all the showering of mouse dropping from my hair, all the

Open Up The Wall

timing of subtrades coming and going, all the building inspections along the way — all these things are easier to bear when you feel some of your heart and soul going into a project. This house was going to be Beautiful, not just "Done."

However, old houses are unpredictable. Phil and I were standing in the bathroom at the top of the stairs, speculating on how long we could keep the toilet functional before we had to remove it to put in a new floor, when Frank appeared at the bottom of the stairs with a coil of plastic rope.

"Here. Use this."

"What for?" I replied.

"Whatever you want. It's a gift. Now, what's going on up there?"

As Frank stomped his way up the stairs, I felt a vibration on the landing and quickly went to the toilet to look inside. Sure enough, there were ripples on the water.

"Spongy floor," I said to Phil.

"I felt it," he said. "Some part of this bathroom is not connected to the wall."

"There goes the toilet," I said. "We'll be peeing down the drain for a few weeks."

We had to take the kitchen ceiling down to see why the floor above was bouncing. Sure enough, the two joists on either side of the toilet had been completely cut away to make room for the toilet drain. There was nothing holding up the corner of the bathroom. I made a note of this in the "Extras" column.

Over the years I have refined a speech that I give to clients about their renovation expectations before I start the work. It is very important that people who have never renovated before know what they are getting into. I don't spare them any of the ugly details about how dirty and disruptive the process can be. I paint an equally scary picture of the surprises that can lurk behind the walls and under the floors of older homes, adding time and money to the bottom line. So when I emailed pictures of the damage to Gene and Lydia, and a price for the repair, they were not taken completely by surprise, and the tenuous trust between client and contractor survived its first hurdle.

Just to be on the safe side, I called the building inspector assigned to this project. Because I had to remedy a structural issue, and because I had never met the inspector for this area, I was leaving nothing to chance. I wanted to establish that I was the by the book, kiss-ass contractor of his dreams. Building inspectors are fair, but demanding people, so I still get a childish sense of dread when I hear their firm authoritative knock on the door. They are like the strict teacher in Grade 5 that you prayed you wouldn't get, because you could never be sure of where you stood with them, because back in Grade 5 you didn't understand power yet. This stuff stays with you.

I booked an onsite inspection for two days later and then Phil and I got to work adding new 2"X10" joists across the width of the kitchen ceiling. We had to cut out the old toilet drain to make room for our new lumber.

Two days later I saw a man in the official hardhat of the building inspector coming up the walkway, so I went out to greet him. When he extended his hand, I

Open Up The Wall

did the same, assuming a handshake. I didn't notice that he was offering a business card and so I continued in handshake mode, bending his fingers back on contact. He winced.

"Oww! What the hell?"

"Oh God! I'm so sorry! I thought we were shaking hands!"

"You really got me! Damn that hurt! Are you the contractor here?"

"Yes."

"I'm Nick. Show me what's going on."

We went to the kitchen and I showed him the new joists. He climbed up on my scaffold and checked that every joist was well secured on the wall plates. He checked the hardware that we had used, measured the distance between the blocking pieces and said, "Good. Let's see upstairs."

I followed him up the stairs and into the bathroom.

He looked down at the torn-out floor. Then he looked into my eyes and said, "I don't see the toilet drain."

"We had to cut it out to make room for the new joists."

"Where's your plumbing permit?"

"Oh shit! I mean ... no. I didn't think to get a plumbing permit. I don't have one. I will get one ... forthwith."

I only kept on blabbing because he kept on staring at me.

Finally he said, "OK. Just get one. And don't try to sneak anything by me or I will come down hard on you."

"I would never do that," I said. "This was an oversight."

"I know. It looks like you care."

I was so relieved, and so grateful for such validation, that I blathered on —"Well, yes, I do care ... and I assure you that I never ..."

"It's OK! Lighten up! I'll see you next for your addition foundation inspection."

He extended his hand and when I went to shake it he quickly withdrew it in mock fear. I laughed way too loud, relieved that he hadn't made me stop work until I got a plumbing permit and delighted that this forced relationship was still working.

I made sure that everybody knew what they had to do and went to city hall to stand in line for a plumbing permit. I didn't bother saying anything like "This had better be done when I get back" to any of them. I finally had a crew that I trusted completely – hard-working, level headed guys with a strong sense of humour, a common dislike of pot lights, and not one tattoo amongst us. They were much older than the kids that I usually hired, so their sense of responsibility was well developed and their experience made them not afraid to take initiative.

"Is everybody happy in their work?" I would ask. "You won't leave me will you? I'll do anything to keep us together ... except pay you more."

We worked the old house over for the first two weeks. She groaned and creaked as we jacked up her staircase and squared up her doorways. We tore down her lath and plaster ceilings and heard the air rushing in from all the cracks in her brick walls. We expelled the vermin that were living between her floors. It was heavy work, noisy, and dirty, and we worked in silence because we were wearing respirators and the dust was

Open Up The Wall

too thick to see across the room.

Then the dust cleared and we got busy putting her back together again, talking and laughing a lot. We discussed the impact of climate change and how to defeat ISIS, but we always found something to laugh about — cruise ships, men's fashion, Starbucks, anything. We patched the old hardwood floors, stripped the old baseboard, replaced the stair treads, tiled the bathroom, and made new closets. Things were on time, on budget, and every week we had something sexy to show our clients.

Except when Phil and I put in the IKEA kitchen.

Cabinets and cupboards were to go on all four of the kitchen walls and there was an island in the middle too, so when the boxes of unassembled cabinets and cupboards and doors and drawers and handles arrived, they took up so much room that the only space we had to assemble them was on the front porch, in sub-zero temperatures. When we finally had the upper cabinets assembled and our fingers thawed out, we discovered that the kitchen walls had such a bow in them that we would have to cut out great chunks of wall in order to make the cabinets hang straight. It took six days to do one kitchen. I saw "The Look" on Gene and Lydia's face for the first time, and I had to fight the feelings of a Geoffrey for the first time in a long time.

We were about twelve days behind schedule and I was a bundle of nerves, fretting more and sleeping less but working longer days, without paying attention to the voice in my head warning me not to rush things. "Keep it together," I told myself. "You haven't fucked up anything — you're just really late. Please don't get insecure and fuck up. Geoffrey. Please!"

Finally, Phil and I had the kitchen screwed in place. There was just one quick thing left to do. I had to move the water pipes two feet to the left. No big deal. Just hurry up. Cut the pipe, heat the pipe, remove the flame and solder. Done it a million times ... but this time I smelled smoke! Sure enough, for the second time in my career, I lit the cupboard door on fire!

I headed off to IKEA for another door while everybody else got their tools out of the house and did the final clean-up. This was the last day for these guys for maybe a month, because I would not need them until the footing was poured, the concrete block foundation was in, and the new addition was framed. Then they would all come back to put in the doors, floors and windows, insulate, drywall and install the finishes — trim, lights, sink, and taps.

I could only hope that they were all still available when I needed them. Their collective good humour and their supportive attitude was as important to me as their skills.

While springtime softened the ground, I made sure that I knew everything there was to know about digging a foundation. Soon, some excavating contractors were going to come by and give me a price. This was uncharted territory for me and I couldn't afford to be caught off guard.

I was in the backyard, measuring and re-measuring the addition dimensions, when I heard:

"No fucking way."

Two fat men came lumbering between the houses towards me. They were the first of the excavators.

Open Up The Wall

These two looked like clowns — big bellies, jowls and high, bald foreheads. I had a sinking feeling. One of them spoke to me in a high-pitched voice.
"How do you expect me to get a backhoe down here? I mean there's no room, know what I mean?" He held out a business card. The address had been crossed out, and so had the office phone number. All that remained was the company name and a cell number.
"Are you saying you have a problem with access to back here?" I asked politely.
"Well figure it out, buddy! There's no fucking room!"
"There's plenty of room," I said. "There's a laneway and a back entrance."
"No way we can get through there with the backhoe! And then where we gonna dump the dirt? This is fucked up!"
"Well, what if the dirt went to the side, wouldn't there be room?"
"Yeah yeah yeah, 'what if.' What if we just take off right now! This whole thing is way too fucked up!"
They turned and walked away. I stood there stunned. Then fatso number one spun around to face me, angrily twirling himself off balance.
"What a fucking waste of my time!" he shouted at me, "You don't know nothing about foundations!"
Something in me gave way.
"No I DON'T! So what? So what if I don't know ANYTHING about foundations? That's why I called you! You're supposed to be the experts! But you turn out to be a pair of whining douchebags!!"
You can pretty much say anything you want to an

obese person because, of course, you can always outrun them.

"We're gone," said Fatso Two. "You can kiss my ass."

"Perish the thought," I said.

"What?" said Fatso Two. "Are you dissing me? Me personally?"

"What do you want me to say?" I fumed. "Thanks for coming to my site and treating me like shit? Get the fuck out of here before I find something to hit you with!"

"You're fucking retarded!" said Fatso One. "C'mon Donnie."

They waddled back from whence they came.

I never used to talk to people like that. I never had that kind of permission in my previous professional environment. What a liberating feeling it is to freely vent my frustration with such abandon! Get it out and get it over with. Flight attendants don't get to do that. Or teachers. Or judges.

NONETHELESS. Fatso's words were ringing in my ears: "You don't know the first thing about foundations!"

Standing in the yard, imagining the addition in place, I let the scope of this project loom ugly in my mind. I imagined the foundation giving way and the addition collapsing into the house and the whole place having to be demolished. All because of some random error in the foundation work that I was too ignorant to catch.

I like to think that all my doomsday scenarios have kept me cautious. I didn't mind over-building structural elements or replacing older material just to be on the safe side. It was worth it to avoid restless nights with

Open Up The Wall

images of disasters wrecking my sleep. For my own peace of mind, I had to finish a project secure in the knowledge that nobody was going to call back with a problem.

Working my way down the list of "Excavation Contractors" in the yellow pages, I was meeting a succession of unqualified backhoe operators, some of whom knew even less about digging a foundation than I did. I got to 'S' and left a message for 'Silvano Construction'.

A soft-spoken man returned my call. "How can I help you?" he said, and I had a good feeling. We agreed to meet on site the next day.

At the appointed time, I met George and his father, who only used his last name — Silvano.

"Best to hand dig this," said George. "It's too risky to swing a backhoe between the fences and the overhead wires."

"Gonna be faster," said Silvano. "We gonna take care of it." And then he patted my arm, which pretty much sold me.

After we made a deal, their first order of business was to get the building inspector Nick to come for a 'meeting.' It turned out that they knew him well. Nick came to the backyard, had a look around, and then we all went off to an Italian bakery for espresso.

There was a level of politeness that would have suited tea with an empress. Subdued tones and napkins on the lap. Casual but formal body language. "Please pass the ..." "Would you care for some ..." Once, George used the word shit and immediately apologized, saying "Excuse my French." The air of regal calm that these gentlemen brought with them inspired confidence.

They arrived early the next morning, and started digging a trench three feet wide by eight feet deep, on three sides of the house. Standing around watching George and his father digging away in the hot sun didn't sit well with me, so over their formal protest I got a shovel and pitched in. I dug for three fascinating days, hearing stories of their family leaving Italy and coming to America. The details of Silvano's family growing strong together in the face of poverty and bigotry was something that a WASP like me is seldom privy to. I pressed them for more personal stories and details and by now, with just their head and shoulders showing in the deepening trench, father and son would call out to me the saga of their family trying to learn English, regretting the move, fearing the future and all crying together as the rain dripped off the roofing nails into the unfinished attic room where they all lived. These sad tales always ended on a positive - "We survived. ... Didn't kill us. ....Made us stronger. ... It wasn't so bad after a while."

We finished late in the afternoon of the third day. The father and son paid special attention to barricading the trench before they left. "Good," said Silvano. "Nobody's gonna fall in there and break a leg."

He had a point. It was a deep trench, made even deeper by the earth that was piled about four feet high on all sides. Now with the picks and shovels gone, it looked more like an art installation than anything to do with construction - unfamiliar, and with a beauty all its own. I slipped under the yellow caution tape and climbed down the ladder to the bottom. A fist-sized

Open Up The Wall

lump of clay rolled from its perch at the top of the pile, bringing more clumps with it as it gathered momentum on its way to the bottom of the trench. I couldn't see what would cause a lump of clay to move.

"Somebody there?" I called. My voice sounded weak, muffled by the dirt walls. I couldn't hear properly. Did someone just run by? The dirt was so high that I couldn't even see shadows. I peered around the corner of the trench. Of course, nobody was there. I sat on the cool earth eight feet below the grass, aware of my discomfort. A long, deep trench is something that few will ever experience anymore. I was picturing all those young, young boys in all those trenches in the first World War. I was getting a sense of how terrifying such sensory deprivation could be in a life-and-death situation. I could see how they accidentally bayoneted each other as they rounded the corners while watching their step in the mud. I could feel how rubbing both shoulders against the sides of dirt walls for weeks on end could drive a soldier out of his adolescent mind.

I wanted to bring my kids over and share this rare strange experience. I wanted this for them, so that when they watched the grainy footage of trench warfare that was broadcast to a new generation every November 11th, it might carry a more visceral meaning in their lives. They were in school, though, and I had to get the concrete footings poured immediately, so I couldn't spare the empty trench for a hands-on history lesson.

George had warned me that his father was very particular about the consistency of the concrete, even going so far as to send a truck back for a better batch.

When our truck arrived, Silvano had the driver pour a small amount of concrete into a wheelbarrow, while he poked at it with a shovel.

"A bit too dry. Get a hose."

I clambered up the side of the huge cement mixer with a garden hose and poured water into the revolving tank until Silvano waved me to stop.

"That's it?" I called. "How can you tell?"

"I just know."

The father and son finished the footing pour while I went to the street to supervise the offloading of the concrete block. The crane truck was on the sidewalk, and already cars were backing up as they crawled around it. I will never understand how the drivers of these rigs remain so calm in the face of the abuse they take. By the time four skids of block was deposited on the front lawn, I was a basket case from directing traffic and smiling and apologizing for the inconvenience as people drove by giving us the finger and calling us names.

"I'm frazzled," I said to the driver. "How do you stay so cool, snarling up traffic all day?"

"I smoke a joint," he said. "Now sign here, I gotta keep moving."

There are thieves who drive around at night in big trucks, specifically targeting construction sites, so I spent the rest of the day moving concrete block to the secure area in the backyard.

Nick, the building inspector, approved the footing, leaving the Silvanos clear to build the block wall. I had hall closets to build in the main house and Trevor, the spray-foam insulation guy, was coming to spray the

Open Up The Wall

main house basement. We were on time and on budget. I was pulling it off. I was running my own show with my own crew.

It was around this time that Ida first showed up.

My friend Gregor, the window manufacturer, called and asked me if it would be alright if Ida came by to look at the bay window we had installed in the front of the house.

"She says she can't tell anything from my brochure, so she wants to see the real thing."

"That's cool, Gregor, send her over."

"She's high-maintenance," he warned. "I can't decide if I like her or not, so just watch your step."

Ida was all business. After we shook hands, she pulled out a notebook and began asking me questions about the window and the installation, writing down my answers. After about ten minutes of this, I told her that I had to get back to work.

"Of course," she said. "Thanks for your time. Oh! I'd like to take a look at your addition. I might want an addition."

She tiptoed through the dirt in her spike heels and I introduced her to the Silvanos, who got out of the trenches and greeted her politely. I clocked her Gucci bag and BMW. It gave me a clue to her taste, and now I knew what kind of windows she would choose.

Finally, the foundation rose up from out of the earth. George cut the final course of block so that it measured exactly 20" above grade. Then I called Nick for the foundation inspection. "Excellent job," he said. "Go ahead and fill it in."

We threw the dirt back in on either side of the new

walls, tamping it down as we went. I jumped and stomped and danced over the loose fill, so relieved that the foundation part of the job was over, and thanking God for the Silvanos.

At the end of the day, I was hosing down the backfilled earth to make it settle faster, when Frank came across the yard, wheeling a bicycle.

"Good job!" he said, and pushed the bicycle at me. "This is for you. I'm supposed to ride it for my heart, but I don't want to. I got pills for that."

The proposed addition was just one storey, at ground level and attached to the back of the main house, so I figured that with the right bunch of guys I could get the whole thing framed in a day. I hired a Portuguese kid and his crew that came highly recommended. Because it was only one day of work, I promised to pay well and to buy lunch. I just had to hope that this was enough enticement for them all to show up.

The afternoon before the big day, Phil and I met the lumber truck and began humping timber and plywood into the backyard.

A man in a subcompact car honked his horn, got out and shouted at us to "Move the goddamn truck". I apologized for the inconvenience and suggested that there was plenty of room for him to get by. It should have ended there, but the man stayed to lecture me on traffic bylaws, shouting yuppie babble like "What gives you the right ...?"

From behind me I heard "You shut yourself up!" and Frank came lumbering off his porch with such fury that the man retreated to his car.

"These boys are working so hard, you little man!

Open Up The Wall

Drive your car away or I will kill you!"

The man made a big show of squeezing past the truck and then raced away.

"You boys get to work," said Frank. "I will look after the cars."

We unloaded and listened to Frank berating drivers for even slowing down.

"Go, go, go! Yes! Lots of room! Then you are a chicken! You are a baby! Go go go!"

When all the lumber was loaded into the backyard and locked up, Frank brought us two tea towels with maps of Russia on them.

"Wipe your faces and then keep the towels for the next time."

It was going to be a long day framing, so I had called for a 7:00 a.m. start. The framers all arrived together, and on time. I showed them drawings, gave brief instructions and then we started putting down the floor joists. Three hours later, it was all down, glued and screwed, and I said: "Good work. Who wants coffee?"

They all looked at each other.

"I'm buying," I said.

They couldn't believe their luck. A boss who bought coffee AND a boss who didn't yell at them. This, they impressed upon me, was unusual.

When the walls were up and braced, I asked: "What do you guys want for lunch?" There was a discussion in Portuguese and Luiz asked: "Could we have Swiss Chalet?"

"Sure," I said.

They stomped on the deck, high-fived each other and shouted "BO - NUS!" These poor guys had hit the motherlode of working conditions ... for one lousy day.

We sat on the new floor and ate chicken dinners. Clesio told me that he and his brother quit school when their dad got cancer and it fell to the boys to pay the mortgage. He had been framing since he was seventeen.

Vic told me that he was 'dyslexic or something'. He had been humiliated by a Grade 9 teacher so he quit school. "As soon as I was out of there," he said, "I finally felt like a man."

After lunch, I let them all have a second cigarette before cracking the whip. "Let's wrap this up in three hours," I said. "I'm getting tired." I didn't tell them that I was worn out and wanted to go home immediately and get into a bath with a bottle of Beaujolais.

There was a breeze when we started on the roof and that helped me. It was getting dangerous to be old and weary, walking across joists, trying to keep up with these kids thirty-five years my junior and their frantic pace. How long had it been since I worked that fast? Time had snuck up on me and I could feel that I was not as strong and not as fast as I was when I was framing with Stan not that long ago. I would have to concentrate on being more careful now to avoid injury.

Finally, as the sun was setting, we stood on the new roof, and I panted, "OK boys, you're done." I handed them each a fistful of cash and we parted company, vowing to work together again.

The next morning, 'my guys' were back. We all had university degrees and none of us had ever known the hardship that the framer boys had. We had known White Boy Hardship, like working overtime to make the student loan payment, but our birthright had spared us

Open Up The Wall 197

the "Grind You Down Until You Are Angry About Everything And Don't Know How To Be Happy Anymore" state of mind that is everywhere in the unskilled trades.

    We began to turn the new addition into a home. We put in the windows and the French doors. Then Phil and I went outside and put up the siding, while Trevor the foam guy came back to spray foam the new walls. Then it was on to the drywall. I had ordered it in 4'X10' sheets. It's heavier to put in place than the standard 4'X8' sheets, but the longer the sheet, the fewer seams there are to tape and cover with drywall mud. That's what I wanted - as few seams as possible, because I have never found the grace and the economy of movement of those real, full-time professional seam tapers. They are a joy to watch, standing on stilts strapped to their calves, swiping a smooth layer of mud over an ugly joint with the graceful arc of an arm, like a heron lifting into flight. By contrast, I am a joke to watch, resembling a rooster furtively pecking at the walls.

    In the end though, my work has a professional finish ... thanks to a lot of sanding. On the final wall, of course I ran out of sandpaper again, so off to Home Depot again.

    Coming out of the parking lot with my "Contractor Pak" of sandpaper, I stopped at the stop sign and was about to turn onto the street when there was an alarming BANG on my passenger door. I couldn't see anything, so I stopped the truck and ran around to the passenger door. I had to look twice. Sitting on the pavement was a real live, one hundred percent clown, complete with red nose, makeup, and baggy polka-dot pants. Beside him was a unicycle. He had a backpack, and I could see oversized clown shoes sticking out of the top. He got to his feet glaring at me.

"Are you alright?" I asked.

The clown mounted his unicycle, adjusted his fuzzy orange wig, and shouted: "FUCK YOU! YOU FUCKING GOOF!" Then he unicycled away down the street.

When I got back, everybody laughed at the surreal absurdity, but we discovered that none of us trusted clowns. They creeped us out, and being so close to finishing this project, an encounter with a clown was akin to having a black cat cross our path. Nobody actually believes in that stuff, but when you work with electricity and water and power tools, disasters can happen and sometimes you find yourself considering omens.

Right on cue, Ida called.

"Are George and his father trustworthy? You say they do good work, and that's one thing, but can I trust them in my home?"

In my calmest voice, I said, "Yes."

"OK great. I'm going to do the basement apartment, so they can have the work, but I want you to put a lock on the main floor door to the basement."

I told Jimmy that I was nervous. "Call her back." he cried. "Call her back and say "FUCK YOU! YOU FUCKING GOOF!"

"It's about ten weeks work."

"Oh. Call her back and tell her that you'll be right over to do anything she asks! Just don't blow this gig!"

It was Jimmy's last day. He was finishing the tile backsplash and then it would just be Phil left to paint the place. We helped him load his tiling gear into his

Open Up The Wall

Porsche, the one luxury item he managed to keep from his high-rolling days in the entertainment business.

There is no group celebration at the end of a full house renovation, because the workers dwindle away one by one as they finish their part of the project. Those left behind get impatient to be done and move on to the next. This time, before we left for good, Phil and I went next door to say goodbye to Frank. He gave us each a packet of Kleenex and a bottle of sparkling water.

"Don't forget me, boys!"

Twenty-Two: Missing the Turn

Self-employment is primarily about keeping yourself employed. As I began taking on bigger jobs, I had to worry about keeping other people employed as well. I wanted to keep this excellent group together, so I was always looking for something good, reasonably long-term and satisfying, for all our sakes. But sometimes, when your eye is on the prize, you look past the red flags.

Ida and I had spoken briefly about her basement apartment ideas. I told her that I would be happy to look at her drawings and give her a price, and that was the extent of our conversation. I was lazy in following up on the conversation and arranging a time to meet. I wasn't remotely excited about getting this job.

At 6:31 a.m. one autumn morning, I was on the beach walking with my dog when my phone rang.

"It's Ida. Are you licensed, and do you have insurance?"

"I am licensed and I have $2 million in liability insurance."

"OK, good. Now I'm going to need a new countertop ASAP, so I'll try you out on that. And while you're here you can look at the plans for the basement apartment."

Try me out? Perhaps the clown was an omen after all. Maybe I should be saying: "Fuck you, you fucking goof!" Instead, I let it go. This was a big job. To have warm dry indoor work for me and my friends all winter long was worth putting up with a bossy lady.

Open Up The Wall

So I went to her house to look at a design plan drawn up by her friend, who definitely was a Fucking Goof.

"This drawing shows your furnace in your bathroom," I said. "That's illegal."

"He wants the furnace beside the shower so it will keep the shower warmer. I think it's a great idea."

"OK, but if you want this to be a legal basement apartment the furnace has to be in a room by itself."

"Alright! Find another place for the furnace! God!"

She fanned her face with her hand, fingers apart, like I had seen those horrible Kardashian women do on TV.

There was a bright digital clock on the counter beside her. After eighteen minutes of me pointing out omissions in her friend's drawings, she conceded that she should send her plans back to the drawing board before I could even think about giving a price.

We made an interim plan. Ida insisted on contracting the Silvanos herself to lower the basement floor. Before the new concrete floor was poured, I would do the layout for all the plumbing fixtures and charge time and material. After the new floor was poured, I was to be given a new design so that I could price the job properly. This was all weird, and ass backward, but at least we were all working.

"In the meantime, I want that countertop in," said Ida. "Just a cheap formica one until the kitchen gets remodeled. How much do you charge for that?"

"The price of the countertop plus $320 labour."

"$320 for labour? Seriously? I can get someone cheaper than that."

"So get them. It's hardly worth it to me anyway."

After three minutes of trying to get the price down, she finally said: "OK, $320. But it better be a good job for that kind of money."

That was the turning point, and I MISSED THE TURN.

When they called to say the countertop was ready, I was making dinner.

I botched a simple stir-fry and had to watch the family chew through the rubbery chicken.

Dixie, of course, saw the mood swing.

"What's going on?" she asked.

"I have a bad feeling. The client is rude and her reactions are a bit off."

"So walk away. That's the best part about your life — you can choose to not take a job. I wish I could."

"Yeah, well, I have to do the countertop and then I'll sort it out with everybody else. It's ten weeks work for the guys. If she's just an anxious homeowner, things will calm down once we get going."

"But you have a bad feeling."

"I'll know for sure tomorrow."

Putting in a new countertop and cutting in a new sink is a job that borders on the mundane, I have done it so often. This time I fretted my way through the job like a novice, double-checking and double-measuring, somehow feeling that Ida would find some fault with whatever I did. I was able to get the job done and get out before Ida got home from work.

On the way home, I was freaked out to see not one, but two clowns standing in front of a sign that said "LAST CHANCE LIQUIDATION SALE!" The clowns waved frantically at me as I accelerated past them, avoiding eye contact.

Open Up The Wall

After dinner, a text from Ida: "COUNTER IS CROOKED!!!!!!!!"

I replied: "Not possible. I will come by tomorrow at 8:00 a.m. OK?"

Ida: "CALL ME IMMEDIATELY PLEASE."

No good was going to come from calling Ida now, because I was furious at her terse, nonsensical message.

Text: "CALL ME IMMEDIATELY!"

Text: "BE HERE TOMORROW AT 8."

I had done a fine job on the counter, so either she was getting ready to stiff me by accusing me of bad work or there was a mental health issue that I would have to deal with. I prepared for both eventualities ... late into the night.

As I was walking up her stairs the next morning, Ida flung her door open. There were two curlers on her forehead. She stomped ahead of me to the kitchen, crossed her arms and glared at me while I checked out the counter.

"Just LOOK!!! You've torqued all the cabinets below the counter. You made them all twist to the left when you put the counter on."

A rage came over me that was frightening. I was furious with myself for ignoring the warning signs, and worse, for getting my friends involved.

I put my 2' level against the kitchen cabinet. It was perfectly level on all sides. I could barely contain my anger at her ridiculous challenge to my work, but I was sure that she was batshit crazy now, so I realized that I had to tread carefully.

I made Ida come over and look at the bubble in the level. "Now we both know that everything is level," I said. "We both know that there is nothing wrong with the counter, and we both know that you are going to pay me now."

"Tears filled her eyes and rolled down her cheeks. "I'm not crazy!! Can't you see? It looks so awful under there, by the drawers."

"Your drawer fronts could have come loose," I suggested. "Maybe they aren't quite level. That might create the illusion of a 'torqued' cabinet."

It was hard to tell if that would have any bearing on her sense of what was level or not. Anyway, I tightened the drawer fronts, raising the top two up a hair, while Ida paced and told me about the bad tradesmen she had encountered – specifically the flooring company she sued for "ruining the hardwood" and the window installer she refused to pay because "he did a crappy job."

"I spent half the year in court with those guys," she said to me.

"I am so out of here," I thought to myself.

I stood back to see if tightening the drawer fronts had made any difference. I couldn't tell.

"You see?" cried Ida, fanning her face with her hand. "You see? Now it's back to normal! My God, how simple was that?"

Ida pranced about the kitchen, thanking me in rapid-fire triplicate, "Thankyouthankyothankyou."

I went straight to the bank to deposit her cheque, as any sane person would.

My phone beeped — a voicemail from a furnace company:

"Hi, my name is Robert. Um ... Ida told me to get in touch with you about setting up a time for a furnace

Open Up The Wall

installation? But, here's the thing. She is, like, weird to get along with? So I talked to my manager? And he says it's OK if I take a pass on this one. Sorry if this screws things up for you. Anyways, have a great weekend!"

Why call me? Was Ida assuming that I WAS going to do her basement apartment, without ever showing me decent plans or discussing a price?

At least it was the weekend. The two sane days of the week when my family comes first, when we catch up on who we are and who the kids are growing up to be. From Friday at 6:00 p.m. to Monday at 6:00 a.m. I don't do business. It's a hard rule to keep. I've had to work at it.

This Saturday morning, the family was scrunched together in a booth at Golden Griddle when my phone went off.

Text: "NEED TO TALK PLUMBING PARTICULARS."

I put the phone on vibrate and we all ordered breakfast.

Bzzzz. Missed call from Ida.

We ate breakfast and talked about nail polish and the Grand Canyon.

Bzzzz. Missed call from Ida.

I ignored it, and we all walked to the park.

Text: "WHERE ARE YOU."

My family waited for me while I stopped and texted a reply: "Unavailable to talk."

Text: "NEED TO TALK."

I suddenly remembered the movie where the crazy woman boils the family's pet rabbit.

When we got home I began drafting my letter of resignation to Ida, even though I didn't technically have a job to resign from. The gist of it was that I was not comfortable with our working relationship. I was careful to lay no blame on her wacky behaviour, saying instead, that sometimes there is a difference in communication style that cannot be reconciled. I told her that I would complete the plumbing layout, as per our agreement. I also said that I would talk to other contractors about giving her a price. That part was a lie.

Text: "CAN YOU CONFIRM PLUMBER CHRIS WHAT'S HIS NAME WILL USE CERTIFIED MATERIALS."

I called Chris.

"Ida wants to know if you use certified material."

"What? What does that mean?"

"Exactly. Listen, I'm going to bail on Ida. The whole situation is getting weirder, and I can't control it."

"Really? I mean she's flakey, but ..."

"No, she's batshit crazy. Maybe bi-polar or something. And I know that she sues, so I'm not going to price her job. I won't bail on you, though. I'll stay until we've placed the drains where you want them, and I'll be there until the Silvanos have poured the new floor. Then I'm done, before she thinks up something to sue me for."

"You really think she would?"

"Totally. Watch your step, pal."

Chris had young children. I began to worry that Ida would find a reason not to pay him.

Text: "ARE YOU THERE?"

Text: "I MUST TALK TO YOU."

Voicemail from Silvano: "Hey, it's George. Ida keeps calling me. She wants to know where you are. Is everything OK?"

Open Up The Wall

I called George back. "Nothing is OK, but here's the important part. I'm going to quit this job."
"What did she do now?"
"Her behaviour is getting crazy, and she sues. Every instinct is telling me not to do business with her. She told me about taking hardwood installers to court, and a window guy is suing her for non-payment."
"Well, OK then. Better to quit than to be in court."
I practically ran to the computer to press send on my letter to Ida. Then I dressed up and went to a dinner party. Luckily it was a large dinner party and few noticed that I was out of sorts, and drank too much.

On Monday morning, I met George and we went in to Ida's together. This is the type of situation where the contractor does not want to be alone with the crazy lady. They publish names of men who are even just accused of rape.

The first thing I told her was that she owed me $1,400 for redoing the design layout, and the corresponding changes to the plumbing, wiring and HVAC schematic. Then I told her that the furnace company that she had called didn't want to deal with her.

Ida kept her eyes on the digital clock. She was squeezing a piece of paper towel, which she suddenly spat on and wiped the clock face.

"I'm not well," she said. "We can talk about this another time."

I was out of there in six minutes and 14 seconds. She never paid me, and I never saw her again.

My relief at getting away without any trouble was tempered by leaving my friends out of work at a bad time of year. With the indoor job now gone, and the leaves already off the trees, the chance of having to work outdoors in winter loomed large. Cold hands, colder feet, icy necks from sweat, icy thighs from leaning against a ladder, holding your pee for way too long to avoid exposing your dick to the sub zero elements, and the constant sniffing make for insufferable days on the job. When I say: "I'm too old for this shit" in June, it's a lame joke, but when I say it from an icy roof in February, it is an ugly fact, no matter how old you are. And crews are just plain bitchier in winter, maybe because of the nagging regret in their heads — *maybe we should have put up with the crazy client and done the inside job anyway, because this sucks!*

We manage to hide our outdoor angst from each other with false cheeriness, and forced smiles. I hate being a part of that vibe, so I came up with a plan.

Twenty-Three: Something Gives

If my plan worked, I could turn things around and get everybody working again.

Pauline and Walt had called in the fall about turning their unfinished attic space into a studio. We had decided on a start date in the spring, when the bare, unheated attic would be neither too hot or too cold to work in. Now, I called them and explained that I had an opening if they wanted to get going immediately.

They agreed without hesitation. What a relief. Everybody had a job up to Christmas and beyond! It's all gooooood.

The plan was to cut a hole in the second floor hallway ceiling and get stairs up to the attic space. Phil and I were covering the hallway with drop cloths and plastic sheets, when I got a call from a network casting office.

"Geoffrey! You are so hard to track down! We have a part for you."

At first I thought it was a joke. With a line like that, who wouldn't?

"Why call me?" I asked. "You should call my agent."

"You kept your agent? For all these years? Great! I'll call her, but while I finally have you, let's set up an audition time."

"Audition? Didn't you just say that I have the part?"

"Nobody has seen you in years, so you have to audition. But the director has asked for you specifically."

"Just me?"

"... And a few others."

This was the exchange that brought it all back – that almost forgotten fear of not knowing exactly where I stood in a business relationship. I lamented the days already wasted, with my life on hold while I waited and waited and waited, hoping that I would be the one chosen.

I chose who to work with now.

"I'm just starting a new project, so I don't see how this could work out," I said. "Thanks for thinking of me, though." And then I went back to work, comfortable that the bridge had been burned without animosity, or remorse.

I had ordered a custom oak staircase from my friend Murray, the one-eyed owner of 'Custom Wood'. Murray had been woodworker until that fateful day when he couldn't find his safety glasses. With only one eye, his depth perception, and therefore his perspective, was too compromised to continue as a finish carpenter, so he brought together a group of genius woodworkers, started 'Custom Wood' and quickly became the go-to guy for custom cabinets, furniture, stairs and railings.

He called with his usual joke. "Come and get your stairs ... I'll keep an eye out for you."

Fourteen heavy oak stairs. From my roster of actors, I hired two tall guys and two short guys to help Phil and I lift them into position. Four of us would hoist the 360-kg staircase from the second floor to the two guys up on the new third floor, who would screw it into place. I watched in slow motion as we strained to push it the final inch into position. "Heave!!" I shouted. "Six inches to go!! Give it all you got!!" And, miraculously, we did it. With back muscles burning, we held it in place until it was screwed into position.

"Well done, crew!" I panted. "Let's get out of here. I'm buying."

Open Up The Wall

Phil looked askance. "It's 2:10 in the afternoon," he said.

"That's right," I replied, "but I can't do any more work today because of this sudden pain in my side, way down low. Get these guys to the pub and I'll be along in a few minutes."

I felt better lying on the floor, but as I slid my hand down the front of my pants, there was this bulge, this bump, this hernia!!

Hernia repair is a surgical procedure, and the recovery time is about two weeks, so a hernia can end up being a costly bit of bad luck for the self-employed. Hernias, strains, sprains, pulls, tears, cuts, bruises ... in the trades, these are occupational hazards.

"It's an occupational hazard," I said to Dixie. "It's not like I did it on purpose."

"What are we going to do?" she said earnestly. "You climb the stairs on your hands and knees, you fall asleep on the couch after dinner and whenever you roll over in bed, you wince. Sometimes I watch you shuffling down the driveway like an 80-year-old."

"My back is good and strong. And I don't need Viagra."

"This is serious!" she cried. "You're 60 years old, climbing on roofs. You're an old man and you load concrete block. No wonder you have a hernia!"

"Jimmy has one too," I said. "All of us have something that hurts. Every single one of us. From time to time, it's unavoidable."

"Unavoidable? What kind of future are you thinking about with an attitude like that? Every time I take out the recycling, there is an empty Tylenol bottle in it!"

"Yes, because I'm managing pain. Not big pain, just

soreness, or stiffness, that usually comes from repetitive movement. Everybody does it. Right now I've got a 30-year-old off work with a sprain. It's a physical job, what can I say?"

"What if you really injure yourself and I end up doing things on my own for the next 20 years, while you watch from your wheelchair?"

The love of my life stood looking at me with anxious eyes, and that upset me. By giving no thought to how my work was affecting her, I had let down my end of our 33-year partnership.

"I haven't thought about it like that," I said, "and I didn't know it was on your mind to this degree. I'm sorry."

"You can take a break between jobs, can't you? Or do smaller jobs? Hire more young guys? We're not going to starve if you don't work so hard. It's time to think about your future."

"I will," I said. "I'm going to go right now and book hernia surgery."

"It's a start."

Twenty-Four: Recovery

I had just enough time before going to the hernia clinic to wrap up some day job/handyman work for some of my longstanding repeat clients. Simple stuff that they could not do by themselves. While there was next to no profit in it for me, I had come to care for these people in their different circumstances, and when I look back on my time as a tradesman I am most proud of helping the people who genuinely needed me.

When Geraldine's husband left her with two small kids, she called me to make her basement a rentable space so that she could hang on to her house. I admired her pride and determination and I was happy to do the work, and throw in some extra hours and a couple of baseboard heaters as well. Whenever she gets a few bucks ahead, she will call me to do the next thing on her repair list. This time it was to replace the broken porch window with one that she had found at a yard sale.

Ten years earlier, I put a deck on Sheila's third-floor walkout. Since then, I have been attending to drafty doors, leaky taps and things that break, because Sheila lives alone, with no handy neighbour or brother with tools to help her out. This time I replaced the screening in her screen door.

Arthur is a 76-year-old art dealer with a heart condition. Two or three times a year I reconfigure his collection and hang the new arrivals on various walls throughout his gallery.

Just a bunch of two-hour jobs for nice people.

"Hi honey, how was your day?"

"Great! After taxes I made $277. 60 and I feel holier than thou."

Mona began shaving me from waist to knee, on my hernia side only.

"You will have your surgery tomorrow morning at 8:00 a.m. The following morning at 10:00 a.m. you will lie on your bed with your pyjama bottoms pulled down to your knees until the doctor comes and examines your sutures. If he is satisfied that you are healing properly, the orderly will walk you to reception, where you will pay your bill and then you will be discharged."

Twenty-seven men and one woman were scheduled for surgery the next day. As we sat down to dinner at round tables of six, I could immediately tell the tradesmen in our group. Their hands gave them away. I talked to a lawyer and someone "in sales," but for the most part I talked to masons, pipe fitters and heavy equipment operators, all herniated in the line of duty. It was my first time in a strange setting where I sought out a pair of rough hands as a way of meeting like-minded people.

Things were a lot less social by noon the next day, with all of us holding our stitches and shuffling about. It was not painful, just uncomfortable, but I complained to Mona that I was in great pain until she gave me some stronger stuff and then I spent the afternoon pleasantly stoned, watching a group of busty women in

Open Up The Wall

a show about real housewives.

"You have a visitor," said Mona, lifting me out of my chair.

I hobbled to the visitor's lounge. There was Stan.

"I can't believe you drove all the way out here!" I said. "Great to see you. They gave me drugs..."

We sat with coffee, and got caught up. It was pretty forced until we began to open up about getting old in the construction business and how much longer we could go on, but neither of us brought up the two-year hiatus, although Stan came close:

"Been a while since we did anything together..."

I wanted to say: *nothing would make me happier than to be working alongside you and your Alpha personality. I've missed our unique camaraderie*, but Stan had always thought that I was too wussy and sentimental, so I just nodded and changed the subject.

"Want to see my scar?"

"It's right beside your dick isn't it?"

"Yeah."

"Then no. Call me when you can walk to a bar."

Twenty-Five: Bloody Hell

My post-op instructions were to walk a lot but not lift anything. On day three, I was shuffling along the sidewalk in front of my house when my neighbour Bob called to me from his rickety front porch.

"How much will you charge me for a new verandah?"

"Off the top of my head ... around 15 thousand."

Bob said, "Good! Let's do it! The mailman won't come up the stairs anymore, now that the railing has broken off. So yeah, let's get going on this."

I was taken aback. "Seriously? Just like that?"

"What choice do I have? It's got to be done."

"Well, OK," I said. "I can't lift anything for seven more days, so you have time to get some other estimates, for your own peace of mind at least."

"I trust you," Bob replied. "And I know where you live, haha."

This was going to be good – working with real wood, outdoors, in the summer AND across the street and two doors down from my own home. I began waking up early with verandah designs on my mind and staying up late working on the graph paper drawings that had to accompany the building permit application - front view, side view and elevation.

The houses on Bob's side of the street were large traditional detached homes, separated by about three feet of mutual walkway. Their vast verandahs spanned

Open Up The Wall

the width of the houses, with high mahogany strip ceilings under a traditional peaked roof. This is why they are called verandahs and not porches. Whole families spent their summers on these grand structures.

I hired Spencer as my helper, because he was tall and the ceiling beams were over eight feet high. He was a bright, positive art school student who loved life, but this wonderful quality was belied by his tone. Even his superlatives sounded indignant. "That looks great" came off as an accusation. "What a beautiful sunset" sounded like there would be trouble if I didn't agree. He was a hard worker, and I think he liked me, but I will never be sure.

We jacked up the roof and supported each corner with a 6"X6" beam, held in place with not one, but two steel posts. This was safety overkill, because I didn't want any crushed children on my conscience. A gang of pre-schoolers had begun collecting on the porch next door to watch us cut up the old porch, and shout Woah!! with each rotted timber that we pitched to the ground below. At any given time there were a few curious kids playing between the houses and hanging around the site for a while, with maybe a nanny somewhere nearby. Safety became a priority, as my imagination kept coming up with images of bleeding mangled kids, so I put up orange plastic fencing to keep the little ones from falling into the fascinating holes that we were digging for the concrete support posts. But the ugly fence drew attention to the job site, which attracted more curious kids, who came with their parents for a tour of the holes and plenty of questions, all beginning with "why." The kids had turned this into a neighbourhood event.

There came a point in this build when I would need some more skilled help to work with me and Spencer. It was only for a few days, so I thought that Stan might be interested.

"Sounds good," he said. "I'll have to come and go a bit, but we can work that out."

He pulled up in his old van and I called from the porch, "Hi Stan." Within seconds, four kids ran from the backyard dressed in plastic armour, carrying popsicles. They all watched him come up the stairs with his huge wooden hammer hanging out of his tool belt slung over his shoulder. Earlier in the day, I had told the kids the tale of a great big carpenter who was coming over to lift the porch roof up, and bash the posts into position with one mighty whack of his legendary hammer. Now Stan was greeted with reverent awe by my young followers.

After introductions all around, we shooed the kids away, placed the new porch posts into their final position and finally took down the steel supports. It felt so natural doing this careful, precise work with Stan again.

When the shadows got long, we tidied up and walked to a patio where we sat in the sun, drank beer and planned the next move, just as we had done for so many years. There was more talk of age, and aches and pains than there used to be.

Stan left for a couple of days after we hung the floor joists, leaving Spencer and me to put down the pine floorboards.

When we were done, I lay face down on the deck and inhaled deeply. This alarmed Spencer.

Open Up The Wall

"What's wrong? Oh God! Are you having a stroke or something?!"
"I'm just smelling the wood."
"What? Why??"
"Because I miss it. I miss doing this. Do you know that I can go for months ... years ... building stuff without using a single piece of natural wood? These days, I build whole kitchens and bathrooms and decks with wood that isn't wood. Cabinetry is all made with MDF – medium density fiberboard, which means pressed cardboard and formaldehyde glue. You can't lie down and smell it because it's toxic. So is plywood and pressure treated lumber and laminated veneer lumber and particleboard and oriented strand board. You have to wear a mask when you cut any of this stuff or you'll get cancer. So I'm lying here and I can feel the warmth of real wood and I can trace the grain with my finger as it travels to the knot, and sometimes I press my initials into the wood with my fingernail ... watch."

Spencer lay face down beside me and took some deep breaths. We lay like that for a few minutes without speaking.

Then he said, "This is pretty chill" and rolled over on his back, resting his head against mine. He raised one tattooed arm, said "Selfie!" and his phone clicked.

The caption on his Facebook post read: "Built this. Taking in the smell of real wood with my boss. Art is in your heart."

When Stan came back the next day, he started work on the stairs while I began on the railings. By 3:30 we were nearly done. The neighbours would be happy if we were to quit early, because I was making a hell of a racket ripping 1X6 pine with my portable tablesaw, the most obnoxious-sounding tool in the carpenter's canon. Now the children were arriving home from day camps and lolling on their porches with their moms and nannies, sucking on slushies. For everyone within an eight-porch radius, the painful shrieking of my tablesaw was destroying the peace of that beautiful summer afternoon.

Aware of this noise intrusion, I was entertaining a weird thought that popped into my head: The inventor of the Seadoo must have taken someone for a test ride, and that someone must have observed that the Seadoo was so noisy that it would ruin a day at the beach for the hundreds of people onshore. Given the number of Seadoos on the water today, the inventor of the Seadoo must have replied, "Fuck 'em!"

Then I saw a streak of blood hit the window beside me.

"Oh no!" I thought. "One of the kids ..."

Then I saw more blood splattered across the untreated pine floor.

Then I saw my hand spurting blood all over the tablesaw.

Even though I wasn't in any pain yet, the visual freaked me out.

"What the fuck? Oh no! Holy Fuck! Jesus Fucking Christ! Fuck!!"

I heard Stan call, "You OK?"

I heard a child shout, "Geoff said the F word!"

I called to Stan, "I've cut my left thumb and I think a finger or two. I can't see for the blood."

"Oh fuck! Oh Jesus! Don't fucking show me! I will throw up!"

Open Up The Wall

From somewhere I heard, "Get in the house, kids."
I shut my mouth and hurried home to wash off the blood and assess the damage. Through the blood spurting out of my thumb, I could see that the whole thumb was still there, so I calmed down a bit. My index finger was like a geyser, so I couldn't tell how much actual finger was left.
As I came bleeding into the kitchen, my daughter gasped and said "I'd better get Mom."
Shame and guilt arrived. "Don't bother her," I said, "I just have to stop the bleeding, then I can put a bandage on."
When I got it under the tap, I could see that I had sliced off the meaty part of my thumb. When I put my index finger under the tap, I caught a glimpse of the finger in two halves, sliced up the middle like a forked tongue, before it was obscured by the profuse bleeding. Suddenly I went from no pain to a lot of pain. From behind me I heard "MOM! DAD'S IN TROUBLE!"
My lucky break that day was that Dixie was working from home.
Trying to sound calm, I said: "I've really fucked things up, I'm afraid. I'm so sorry, but can you to take me to the hospital?"
Her face went from alarm to all business. In no time, there was a clean towel around my hand, and we were heading to the hospital.
"Just drop me off," I said. "You can't park anywhere around here, so drop me off and I'll be fine."
"Shut up."
The big-assed paramedic at the check-in was busy flirting with the skinny paramedic with the wispy

goatee, so she told me to take a seat. Dripping a trail of blood, I headed to the waiting area. No sooner had I sat down, when the people on either side of me got up and moved away, leaving me overcome with shame. I had been careless, and now I might lose my finger. What a loser. What a Geoffrey! I hadn't thought about Geoffrey in a long time. What a weird thing to be thinking anyway. I couldn't even figure out what had gone wrong yet.

"Why is my husband sitting there bleeding? Why hasn't he seen the triage nurse yet?"

Dixie was here.

In no time flat, she had me registered and I was sent for an X-ray, where it was revealed that the bone in my index finger was ground up as far as the first knuckle.

Dr. Kim came in and looked at my fingers. She had long delicate fingers, with her nails cut very short.

"I'm going to sew you back together," she said. "Follow me."

In a thin voice I asked, "Can my wife come too?"

Lucky for Dr. Kim that she said, "I guess so."

We went into an operating room that appeared to be part storage area. There were boxes piled and a wall of cabinets and drawers. I lay on the operating table under a huge light.

Turn your finger towards the light," said Dr. Kim.

"I can't see the light."

"What?"

"I have my eyes closed."

"Oh, for heaven's sake! Open your eyes and turn the inside of your finger toward the light."

"No!"

"OPEN THEM!"

Open Up The Wall

"NO! I don't want an image of this split finger to ever be in my consciousness! EVER!! I'm keeping my eyes shut!"

"I can turn his finger for you," Dixie said.

"Wash your hands, then and put on some gloves," said Dr. Kim. "And a mask. And bring me more gauze pads. They're in the top middle drawer."

I kept my eyes shut while the two of them worked. Dixie twisted my hand this way and that while Dr. Kim sewed.

With one hand easing mine into position, and one hand moving the light to where Dr Kim commanded, Dixie's contribution was the reason things got sewn up so quickly, thereby avoiding the risk of bone infection, which would have necessitated cutting off my finger at the first knuckle.

"I'm going to need another needle to get through the fingernail," said Dr. Kim. "Bring me that sterile tray there."

"Are you actually going to sew right through his fingernail?" asked Dixie.

"Stop talking!" I commanded. "I don't want to know! I don't want to even imagine that!"

They stopped talking. I thought I heard a titter.

Twenty minutes into the procedure, I said: "I can feel that."

"This is a bigger job than I anticipated, so the freezing is wearing off," said Dr. Kim.

Five minutes later, I asked if I could have some more freezing.

"No. We're nearly done here."

"It really hurts!"

"Four more sutures," said Dr. Kim.
"Make it two," I bargained.
"Four!" said Dixie. "You can take it."
And I did. And then it was over and Dr. Kim removed her gloves, said "bye bye" and hurried back to the emergency room. She didn't even leave a space for me to say thank you.

At home, I sat in the kitchen looking at the fat bandages on my thumb and forefinger while Dixie mopped dried blood from the hallway, the sink, and the kitchen floor.

"Do you remember what Dr. Kim said about the home handyman?" she asked.

"No, because I made a conscious effort not to listen to you two talk about bones and needles and infection. I sang songs in my head."

"Well, she said that your average weekend handyman doesn't have accidents like this because they never lose their fear of their power saws. It's only you pros who get casual and slice yourselves up. Does that fit with what happened to you? Do you know what went wrong?"

"Sure. I should have lowered the saw blade from 3" to 1" before continuing on with the narrower cut. My brain had geared my fingers for a 1" high blade, but they ran into a 3" high blade. That's it in a nutshell, but the fact remains that I got cut by a stationary saw, which can only mean one thing – I was careless. I am so sorry to put you through all of this. I'm ashamed of myself. I feel stupid."

I felt a bit better the next day after fielding calls of support and encouragement. Stan called and told me about the time he sliced his thumb right through to the

Open Up The Wall

tendon. Then Rick called and told me about shooting himself with a nail gun, and how they had to take him to hospital with a drawer nailed to his hand. Then Davey called to tell me how he almost cut his fingertip off, but it didn't cut right through so, realizing that it was too far gone to be saved, he put his finger back on the saw and finished the job. Michael told me about the burns he got lighting his leg on fire with sparks from a metal saw. And then Ken called to say that I was lucky to have got this far in construction without killing myself, because I was "such a fucking dipshit."

"I mean, remember when you hit your own head with your own hammer? That's fucking dumb, right? So ... power tools ...well, you're lucky you're still alive and you still got a finger, right? At least you're going to look like a carpenter now."

So now I was part of a club. Being in such company helped me feel better about being such a fucking dipshit.

Stan spent the next three days finishing the porch for me, then he carried all of my tools back to my house, including the table saw caked in blood. It was so offensive to the eye, and to the memory, that I hosed it down and donated it to an overseas aid organization.

Images of the event continued to arrive unannounced in my mind. A close-up picture of my finger spurting blood all over the picture window would suddenly appear and then, just as suddenly, disappear. I thought of all the soldiers and cops and front-line workers with much more horrible, traumatic images trapped in their heads, upending the rest of their lives, and I counted my blessings.

Twenty-Six: Process of Elimination

"There's always something to be grateful for," said Li as she pushed my twisted finger into my palm. "You are lucky you still got this finger."

Li, the physiotherapist, was trying to regain some mobility in the end joint of my finger now that the stitches were out. My first impression of her had been a soft-spoken young lady with kind eyes and a demure, pursed smile. She was very gentle, and really sweet, right up to the moment that she put my hand on her therapy table. Latching onto my finger with her right hand, she literally bared her teeth as she forced my hand onto the table with her left hand. Once restrained, she had her way with my poor finger, bending it and twisting it all the while wearing a nasty scowl on her face. Twice a week I was subjected to her torture. I tried to weasel out of the last few sessions.

"It's kind of a losing battle, don't you think, Li?"

"Don't say that!" she said, bending my finger painfully forward. "You will get mobility back, IF YOU DO YOUR STRETCHING EXCERCISES!!!" She shouted directly into my face.

"OK! You don't have to yell in my face!"

"It is necessary sometimes. You are squeamish. You are the worst kind of patient. You try to avoid pain by NOT DOING YOUR STRETCHING EXERCISES!!!"

"Oh for God's sake, Li! I do all of your exercises every day! Fat lot of good it does, though. I still can't make a fist

Open Up The Wall

properly, and I have no feeling in my fingertip."
"You're pretty old, so it's going to take longer."
"Seriously? C'mon, I'm not that old."
"Hah! Look at yourself! You are above average age to be working in construction. You will sustain more injuries in the next five years than you have in your whole working life – sprains, torn ligaments, lower back pain, arthritis ... it's all coming your way. You're not stupid. Surely you must know that."
"I've never thought about it. I don't feel old enough."
Li pushed my finger to my palm until I winced.
"Then think about all the repetitive movements you do. I can tell by the way you walk that your left knee will be the next thing to go, from all the up and down. And by the way you take off your jacket I can see that there is probably a muscular/ skeletal issue going on in your neck. Want me to take a look?"
"No way. You like hurting me too much. I appreciate the lecture, though."

First the hernia and now the finger. For the second time in a year, I was out of work because of injury. Nobody else that I knew had such bad luck. But was it bad luck? Or was it something in me? I wasn't the clumsiest, but I was certainly the oldest of my peers ... by 10, 20 or 30 years, depending on the crew that I was working with. Li's warning about the inevitable toll that construction work takes on the body would not leave my mind. There was no denying that some of my pain was now chronic, so I couldn't completely dismiss her professional opinion — much as I wanted to.

I kept on working, beautifying the city one house at a time and enjoying life with my professional friends. I finally had an image of myself that I liked, one that had grown out of my life as a builder of things that please people. Still, my split finger didn't work and I couldn't lift much weight above my head with my left arm. It probably wouldn't hurt to take some time off. But then Mrs. Pearson called about three new doors and I never say no to repeat clients, so I put off taking time off to do the doors. And then Sheila broke her outdoor tap, so I ran a new pipe through her basement wall and hooked up a new one. And then a new client wanted a wooden grid built for his living room ceiling and it was such a unique build that I couldn't say no, and so I ended up with a herniated disk in my neck.

"It happens at your age," said Marcio, the X-ray tech.

"I keep telling everybody, I'm not old. Not that old."

"OK, sir. If you say so."

I lay on the X-ray table while Marcio positioned my chin.

A terrible thought entered my mind and sent a shiver through my body: my best before date has arrived!

I had to come to terms with my shelf life. I had loved ones who needed me for more than just a paycheque.

Know When to Fold 'Em.
Quit While You're Ahead.
Let Jesus Make The Call.

The speaker on the ceiling squawked "Take a breath and hold it" and I gasped in a breath, not because I was instructed to but because I was suddenly startled by a vision of me at a flea market, selling my tools from the back of the truck.

No severance.
No pension.
Slow death as a Walmart greeter.

Twenty-Seven: Going South

"How old are you?" asked Rick.
"I'm 62."
"HOLY FUCK!! I had no idea! Are you on Viagra?"
The best present that I got for my tenth birthday was a picture book called Greek Mythology. The Adonis and Aphrodite myth was preceded by an amateurish painting of a handsome muscular youth, deeply tanned, with severe aquamarine eyes and blond hair blowing in the wind. At his feet sprawled a big-breasted Aphrodite, looking up at him with hearts coming out of her eyes. When I first met Rick, I was startled by his resemblance to the Adonis painting. Whenever we were together, I was aware of women watching him, but I never teased him about it because Rick could turn on you. Today, he was all smiles at the chance meeting of me and Stan in the Home Depot parking lot.

The clouds were in high-definition contrast against the bright blue sky, but it wasn't crisp enough for a jacket so Stan bought us coffee and the three of us sat on the tailgate of my truck, swinging our legs and catching up on each other's summer. Rick was a licensed carpenter half my age. I had been in awe of his meticulous work as a cabinetmaker from the beginning, and I was always quick to volunteer as his lackey whenever he showed up on the same job as Stan and I. Once, early on, I made a point of thanking him for all the woodworking fundamentals that he had taught me.

"You learned from the best, because I learned from

the best," he said. "Now you have to keep up with me and Stan and keep getting better, or we'll set you up with a 'Fuck It, That'll Do' crew."

How lucky that Geoffrey had fallen in with men who took pride in their work, who paid attention to detail, and were, above all, honest. How awful to think that it could have gone the other way and naïve Geoffrey could have fallen in with a 'Fuck It, That'll Do' crew. I fought the urge to tell them how much I liked them.

Geese were honking overhead and I watched groups of men across the parking lot pause their loading of materials to watch the noisy birds practise getting into their V formation. Perhaps 20 men looked to the sky, shielding their eyes from the sun with their hands, watching the flight rehearsal. A self-conscious cheer came from the crowd when the geese finally got it right and flew out of sight, honking.

This little gap in our lives lasted less than a minute. We all watched the event, felt something amazing and then went back to our realities. Concrete blocks thumped into vans, lumber slapped into pickups, male voices filled the air, laughing, shouting, moaning and groaning. I put on my glasses to see their faces. Some looked as old as me, some looked happier than me, some looked angrier, some cooler. There were young men limping, and middle-aged men coughing.

To neither one in particular, I asked: "What's going to happen to all these guys?"

"They're all gonna have heart attacks right here in the fucking parking lot because they're too fucking old to be working!" Rick shouted at me. "Jesus, Geoff! You worry too much. So shut up!"

Open Up The Wall

Stan had been present years earlier when Rick's father called his son "a useless piece of shit." Rick had been dealing with anger and self-esteem issues ever since I had known him.

"It's a big question," I said. "Think about it. We don't have mandatory retirement. We don't have company pension giving us incentive to retire after 30 years. Nobody is going to organize a celebration and give us a gold watch and wish us good luck in the future. So? What happens to us? Do we pick a random date, say 'I quit' and then sell our tools the next day? Or will something happen, and we just won't feel like going to work anymore?"

"I feel that way now," said Rick.

"I'll stop when I have to have my knee replaced," said Stan. "I've got a few years yet. I'll be about your age by then."

"So the decision will be made for you."

"I think you're making too much of it right now. You're in good shape, except for your neck and your finger."

"I only think about it when I'm sore," I said, "And when my wife watches me – the way I get out of a chair, the way I climb stairs. I feel guilty about messing with my future, because I'm messing with hers too.

We sat in silence, watching the sky. Stan massaged his knees. I did neck rolls.

A subcompact car began to pull into the parking space beside my truck, right under the sign that said CONTRACTOR PARKING.

Rick sprang from the tailgate, and stepped into the path of the little car. He banged on the hood and shouted at the windshield:

"THE SIGN SAYS CONTRACTOR PARKING!! YOU ARE NOT A FUCKING CONTRACTOR!! WE NEED THESE SPACES FOR LOADING OUR MATERIAL, SO GET THE FUCK OUT!! IN YOUR STUPID FUCKING CARDIGAN!!! GET! OUT!"

We watched the little car back out and drive away. Rick ambled back to the truck, fixing his gaze on Stan and me. Then he took an elaborate bow.

"You're welcome," he said. "Somebody has to keep the civilians out of here, RIGHT?"

Stan and I muttered embarrassed thank yous.

"You're welcome," he replied sarcastically. "Hey Geoff, why don't you go inside and offer to be the Home Depot parking attendant? They hire lots of old washed-up contractors. The aisles are full of them."

"Perfect," said Stan. "I could panhandle at the entrance in my wheelchair, and you could run me off the property."

"How about the sex trade?" Rick offered. "You could make some money off all those old broads moaning over guys in tool belts."

As I looked at Rick, it hit me hard that if I were to walk away from this business, I would never see him again. Life would not offer up such extraordinary characters outside of this work environment.

We sat in silence again. Then I said: "You'll understand this, Stan. Since I started working as a contractor, I don't see me the way I always saw me. I have a completely different image of myself."

"From actor to renovator. It was bound to happen."

"It goes deeper than that. I can't think of any job where I could see the smile on someone's face, and

Open Up The Wall

hear them say 'I love it' and 'Thank you' and even give me a hug sometimes, all because of something I did. That's what changes a person."

Rick sighed and put on his sunglasses.

"You sound like a fucking Care Bear."

"What do you expect?" demanded Stan. "His mother abandoned him when he was a baby."

"Yeah!" I said. "And Stan's mother wrecked Christmas! We need to feel the love!"

"My dad smacked me around a lot," countered Rick, "but you don't hear me talking like you guys. You guys are fucking weird."

"But you still love us. Right?"

Rick struck the 'God give me strength' pose – arms open, eyes rolled heavenward.

"Kiss my ass, you fucking has-beens."

We watched him go.

"The most down-to-earth psychopath I ever met," I said.

"If you wind down, what will you do with your repeat clients? Are you going to cut them loose?" asked Stan.

"I hadn't thought about them. You can have them if you want them. Some of them depend on me though, so I won't let those ones down."

"So, you're talking semi-retirement?"

"I don't know, I don't have a plan. At this point, I'm just ... trying to imagine the finale."

"Yeah, I think about it. Anyway, gotta go."

Walking to the recycling bin with the coffee cups, I watched one of the laces on my worn-down boot slowly come undone. Every day I wore work boots. Every day I ate a sandwich with dirty hands, sitting amongst my small fortune of tools. My truck always had material in the back, destined for greatness in somebody else's home.

I was the opposite of what I had been brought up to be, and that made me happy. In that sense, I had fulfilled a dream.

I remembered Greg with his crooked grin and his tongue-in-cheek pronouncement "It's all about people helping people" and I remembered how Stan and I had laughed.

Walking back to the truck, I saw Stan's van. I could see his face in the side mirror.

"Are you spying on me?" I asked.

"Yes. I'm worried that your anxiety about your future is severe enough that you will try to take your own life."

He got out of his van and made the usual three or four tries before the door shut properly.

"I can't read how serious you are about stopping," he said. "You're being such a drama queen about your future that I don't know if I should even bring this up, but I've got a big one lined up — a second-floor bedroom turns into a huge bathroom and the existing bathroom turns into an office AND lots of custom woodwork ... floor-to-ceiling closets, with shelves and shoe racks.

"I'm in," I said.

"Just like that?"

"Just like that."

And just like that, I was excited again.

We did the job, we had fun with the sub trades as they came and went, we all drank beer after work and talked about our kids, our portfolios, and sometimes we talked about what else we could do with our lives before we died ... just like we always did.

When the job was over and I had humped the 614 lbs.

Open Up The Wall

of tools back down to my basement, Dixie and I went to Holland. Then we canoed Lake Superior. I sold a few of the tools, just to make more room in the truck.

Rick developed carpal tunnel syndrome, so he took a job teaching carpentry at a community college. In his first semester, he was called before the dean and told to stop using expletives. His response was that this was normal speech in the trades, and if they didn't like it they could go fuck themselves. He remained on faculty.

Ken went back to jail for parole violation. Something to do with a knife fight. None of us even knew that he was on parole, or what for.

Phil's body type made him prone to back injury, so when it started to act up after helping me carry drywall through a snow-covered back yard and down the stairs to a basement reno, he started a painting company.

Jimmy's wife got a job, so he was able to slow down a bit and only do work for his friends.

Silvano and his beloved wife spend half their time at their farm in Italy, leaving George to run the business. Without fail, we all get together when he is in town, and every Christmas they bring me a present.

Stan got in touch with his agent again, and started getting work on TV in the 'older man' roles.

After twenty years of helping other people, I finally got down to working on my own houses. The stairs don't squeak anymore. The rotting deck is replaced and, at last, the kitchen has a new ceiling. I still spend a lot of time and money at Home Depot.

But I don't park in CONTRACTOR PARKING anymore.

Acknowledgements

I had always thought that writing a book must be a lonely, solo endeavour. It turns out that it is a collaborative effort. I know that this book would never have happened without the support and encouragement from some very special people.

The first person I told that I was trying to write a book was the actor Dixie Seatle, who is also the love of my life, my partner of 44 years, and the mother of our children. Every weekend I would make Dixie listen to what I had written that week, and wait for her observations. These observations, and her encouragement kept me writing through the week every night after work.

When I had written 40 pages, my friend and playwright David Bolt demanded to have a look. For months after that, David badgered me to keep at it, "What's your page count now? Keep writing no matter what!" He saw the completed first draft a week before he suddenly died.

His widow, author Sarah Sheard picked up where he left off, and for well over a year she was my mentor and guide through the writing world, teaching me everything from how to format a manuscript, to how to write a synopsis. No matter how stupid my questions, she was always calmly there for me.

My cousin, Brian Reid had a strong professional background as an editor, and he took it upon himself to spend days going through my manuscript, editing out thoughts that went nowhere, fixing typos and grammatical errors until the read was seamless.

Jane Gibson and her husband Barry Penhale, are well known veterans in the publishing business, and without my even asking, they offered to have a look at my manuscript and give me the benefit of their experience in the field. They were the ones who introduced me to audio producer Tim Reilly, owner of Leaking Ambience Studio. Tim is the one person responsible for taking the words from my laptop and turning them into the book that you are reading now. This is a hugely detailed, technical task, and Tim spent many hours alone in front of two screens formatting the ebook and then the hard copy edition, all the while maintaining his great sense of humour.

Acknowledgement in the context of this journey, seems … formal. I love these people for involving themselves with me, and my collection of thoughts. Asking nothing in return, they helped me through the uncharted territory of getting words on a page to market, and in doing so, they became a wonderful part of my life. I am deeply grateful to each one of them.

About the Author

After graduating from the National Theatre School of Canada, Geoff Bowes enjoyed a successful career as an actor, working across North America, garnering awards and critical praise. He performed on stages across Canada, starring in premier productions by his friends George F Walker, Erika Ritter, and Dave Carley. He guest starred in all of those TV shows of the 80's and 90's – Street Legal, Top Cops, Night Heat, Wind at my Back, Goosebumps, etc. Film work took Geoff from Los Angeles to Montego Bay, co-starring with many Hollywood luminaries. The nice ones included Bruce Dern, Ann Margaret, James Woods, Farrah Fawcett, and Tom Sizemore.

Like so many of his actor peers, Geoff found it increasingly difficult to accept the lack of autonomy in his life. After 25 years of auditioning and taking direction, he signed on with a construction crew, and reclaimed his soul by working with his hands. As a carpenter, he was exposed to a host of awe inspiring characters, on both sides of the toolbelt, and he started to write about them, drawing on his experience in dramaturgy to bring many of them to life through dialogue.

Like so many of his contractor peers, Geoff's exit from the construction business came as a result of injury, and chronic pain. After eighteen years as the hands on owner of his construction company, he shut it down, and moved to his farm in Markdale, Ontario, where he lives with his beloved wife, his devoted dog, and a herd of indifferent cows.

Manufactured by Amazon.ca
Bolton, ON